D1031601

DAVID W. BERMANT

THE AUDACIOUS ART COLLECTOR

DAVID BERMANT FOUNDATION

© David Bermant Foundation 2012

All rights reserved. No part of this publication may be reproduced, stored in a retrieval
system, or transmitted, in any form or by any means, electronic, mechanical, photocopying,
recording, or otherwise, without the prior permission of the publisher.

Compiled by Katherine Boone

Edited by Susan Hopmans

PHOTO CREDITS

Blanka Buik

Charles Erickson

Stephen Gerberich

Jean-Pierre Hébert

Susan Hopmans

Miu Ling Lam

Anne Niemetz

Brad Rochlitzer

Alejandro & Moira Siña

Joseph Szaszfai

Ethan Turpin

Victoria Vesna

Produced by

Sea Hill Press Inc.

www.seahillpress.com

Santa Barbara, California

Printed in Hong Kong

A lover of kinetic art,

the kind that will pulse like a heart.

He could not get ecstatic

over art that was static.

Liked the kind that would stop and then start.

WALT HOPMANS

AUGUST 27, 1993

DEDICATION

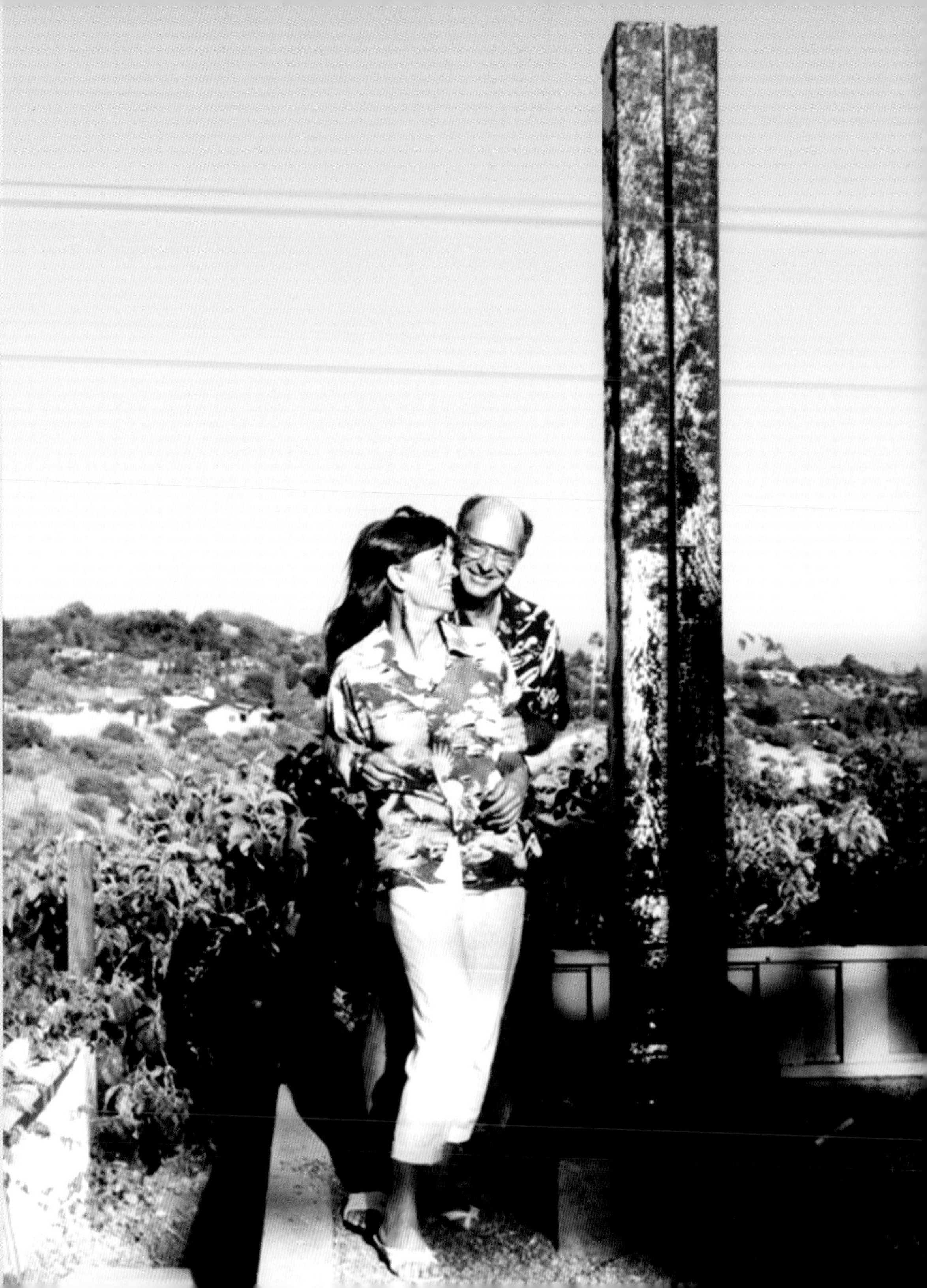

This book is dedicated to the very lively memory of the fabulous David W. Bermant. He was the love of
my life. Being his best friend and wife was an unbelievable honor. One of his favorite sayings was,
"I love wine, women, and art—and not necessarily in that order."

I would say he loved life and lived it to the fullest. He was a brilliant
bundle of contradictions that made him such a fascinating person.
One never knew exactly what he was going to do or say.

He had many friends, and he was so very generous. The planet was lucky
to have had him for his brief eighty years.

He wanted to be remembered after he was gone,
and I hope this book will do that in a big enough way to satisfy him.

SUSAN HOPMANS

DAVID WILLIAM
BERMANT
1919–2000

IN MEMORIAM

David Bermant was a longtime good friend of mine as well as my son-in-law. We agreed and also disagreed on various points of philosophy as well as art. Mostly we agreed, and when we didn't, we needled each other mercilessly and laughed a lot. The man's sense of humor seldom left him.

David's two great interests were building shopping centers—which he did with enthusiasm and success both on the East Coast and in California—and collecting art. The art dearest to his heart was of a technological nature. The title of one of the several major shows he sponsored, P.U.L.S.E. (People Using Light, Sound, and Energy), is a clue to the sort of unique work he felt was the art pertinent to our time. It was art that utilized modern science and technology and did something other than hang on a wall or stand on a pedestal. And he felt that such art should be shown in public places, not just in museums and galleries.

Many pieces from his extensive collection are on loan or contributed as gifts to the City of Santa Barbara and to UCSB. At the airport, in the County Building, in the main library, in public schools, and at several locations on our beaches can be seen examples of his unusual, colorful, moving art pieces. To make sure the art form he loved should continue to flourish beyond his lifetime, he established and funded the David Bermant Foundation: Color, Light, Motion.

First came love, then came marriage, then came David in a baby carriage.

Ruth

David was born in New York City, grew up in Manhattan, and, at twenty-one, graduated cum laude from Yale University. Six months later, in January 1941, he volunteered to join the U.S. Army. Starting as a private, he ended his army career as a major of artillery in Patton's Fifth Army, earning a bronze star with an oak leaf cluster for his actions. In 1947, he married Ruth Josephson, and they had four children: Ann, Jeffrey, Wendy, and Andrew. After forty-six years, they were divorced. David then married Susan Hopmans and they established a home in Santa Barbara as well as in the Santa Ynez Valley. Here he created facilities for and maintained a large collection of the art he felt was so significant.

I knew David Bermant as a man who had a great capacity for enjoying the material as well as the aesthetic pleasures of life. A connoisseur of food and wine, he once flew to Paris to participate in a special gourmet event and flew back within twenty-four hours. He delighted in fine cigars until he realized that good health would be an even greater pleasure.

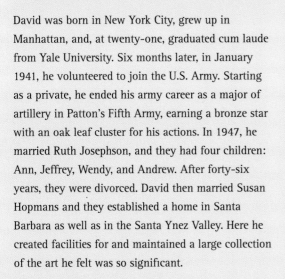

David could be tough when circumstances required, but his sense of humor was never absent. Even during his terminal illness, he was able to make wry jokes about the situation. A vital part of his personal philosophy came from discussions he had had with a Yale professor he admired, F.S.C. Northrop. They pondered the big questions of what is "right," what is "wrong," and what is "truth." In a letter summarizing the conclusions he reached, he wrote to me: "I think one can find truth for one's time. One can find right and wrong for one's time. Maybe none of these are eternal, but they are to be found. I'm going to try to seek out the truth as long as I live and always tell the truth as long as I live, not only to others but mostly to myself. I will never lie."

Staying true to that difficult agenda may well be a bit part of the reason for his long, happy, and successful life.

Left to right:

DWB
....
DWB with Dad & brother
....
DWB at bar mitzvah
....
DWB with parents
....
DWB in U.S. Army

Lou Zona
Executive Director
Butler Institute of American Art

DAVID WILLIAM
BERMANT
1919–2000

ABOUT DAVID

David Bermant was a visionary. How else would you describe a man who saw great and significant art dwelling within the world of technology?

Before anyone considered technologically based artistic expression as serious art—there was David Bermant. Not only did he come to recognize that art created with light or digital electronics was indeed on the same level as painting or sculpture, he took the unprecedented step of actually acquiring such work and encouraging artists to stay with their vision and to continue to explore new realms.

I was introduced to David Bermant by the renowned art dealer Ivan Karp, who described David Bermant as one of the truly great collectors of our time. Ivan knew of my affection for art based on technology and of my interest in one of his artists Clyde Lynds, who pioneered the use of fiber optics in sculpture. I eventually met David at Ivan's OK Harris Gallery in New York, and we immediately were heading toward Lynds' studio on Long Island. Walking into that space-age artist's studio with David was an amazing experience. David's excitement in sharing this experience was only topped by his enormous admiration for what Clyde Lynds had achieved. He could not have been more enthusiastic for the work had Clyde been his son. That visit with David and Clyde, and the subsequent drive to David's home in Rye to see part of his collection there, was an experience that I will never forget. Although most of the artists were not known to me at that time, David walked me to each piece, demonstrated its unique qualities, and discussed each artist as if he were describing Rembrandt or Degas. As I listened to each descriptive word, it became clear to me that David Bermant truly understood the aesthetics of each work and believed totally in the creators of each piece. As I think back on that day, I believe that I grew as a museum and art professional. It was my first step in coming to appreciate that serious and important art was being created off of the main street and by artists who took risks in new and exciting technological media. At that time they performed before an audience of one: David Bermant.

One of my proudest moments as director of the Butler Institute of American Art was hosting one of the first comprehensive exhibitions of the Bermant collection. It was an eye-opener for most museum visitors who had never experienced art that looked and acted that way. This was also the impetus toward the creation of an art and technology wing, the Beecher Center, here at the Butler Institute, which was funded by the state of Ohio and a local community foundation, the Beecher Foundation. But a key part of this unique venture was the creation of a gallery equipped to handle any and every type of technologically based artwork, the David Bermant Gallery. Nothing could have been more appropriate than to name a gallery of visionary art after the greatest visionary of that artistic genre, David Bermant.

(continued on page 10)

DWB with John Harris' "Mirrored Dome"

....

DWB with Nam June Paik's "Participation TV"

....

DWB with knopkierie he got from Zulu warrior on African safari

....

DWB with knopkierie

(continued)

Much has been said about those qualities that make up the ideal collector. The term "passion" is invariably used to describe the collector's primary personality trait. With David Bermant, it certainly was a passionate pursuit, but it was more than the satisfaction of a need to possess things. With David, it was a cause to be shared. When I asked him to display his extensive and varied collection with us, I saw a side of him that endeared him to many. He saw in my invitation the opportunity to expose a new kind of art to yet another audience. The night of the opening reception, he became an evangelist, preaching and educating everyone in the galleries as to the wonders of what these artists had achieved. I can still see him demonstrating the interactive work by Nam June Paik, an artist whom David admired and championed early on. His devotion to the cause of new and exciting media won over many that very night, making our future efforts to present a permanent home for technologically based art at the Butler Institute much easier to accomplish.

It is certainly no wonder that the artists collected by David would have such great affection for the man. Over the years, the Butler has shown numerous Bermant artists in the museum's Bermant Gallery, and with each exhibition comes a tribute to the singular vision of this extraordinary man. It is clear that the artists who experienced David's encouragement and support remain committed to the ideals of David Bermant. Even though David has been gone for some time, his adventurous spirit seems to be alive in the artists who first inspired him and, in return, inspired. But I am convinced that David would be thrilled to know that another generation of artists has taken the banner and are running with new ways to marry art and science. He would be overjoyed at what has transpired as a result of digital technology being available to the artistic mind. He would be ecstatic to know LEDs have advanced so dramatically, and that computers and large-scale digital printers are offering images with such clarity as to be unimaginable just ten years ago.

That ever advancing technologies would one day become a tool of the artist would have been unthinkable just a few years ago. But David Bermant saw this. He envisioned a world of art that dazzles us visually while challenging us intellectually. The future of the artist, as David Bermant predicted, would be intrinsically tied to the scientist. David applauded this collaboration and devoted a great deal of his life to permitting it to flourish. His vision and his good work will live on through the ongoing creative energy within the artists whom he discovered and promoted, and through the spark of innovation found within a new generation of artists who are, and will be, inspired by what he was about. Thank you, David Bermant, not only for what you once accomplished, but also for the impact that you continue to have on us. You introduced us to a universe of new ideas, and in the process enriched our lives and stimulated our imagination as to what the future of art may become.

February 17, 1970

Dr. F.S.C. Northrop
245 Whitney Avenue
New Haven, Connecticut

Dear Dr. Northrop,

I am hopeful that you remember me as one of your former students, upon whom you made an enormous impression. To aid your memory, I took your basic logic course in my freshman year, and then your philosophy of science course, which you only spent six months teaching us, as you went on a sabbatical.

I have been an avid, although not always understanding, reader of everything you have published since my days at Yale, and quite frankly, I continue to base my philosophy of life around the tenets which I intuitively gathered from you. I say "intuitive', because I sometimes doubt the ability of my intellect to comprehend some of your thoughts, but I think I get them nevertheless.

Since my days at Yale and service in the Army, I have been developing shopping centers in different parts of the United States, including Hamden Plaza, which I hope you and your family occasionally patronize in Hamden (if your wife shops at Richard Thomas in that center, tell her to mention my name to Mr. Thomas, and she'll get very special treatment).

At the present time, I am building enclosed mall centers of much greater size than the Hamden Plaza, and I am decorating the interiors of the centers with examples of contemporary art, rather than the usual landscaping and fountains employed by my competition. In order to have a meaningful representation of contemporary art, I have chosen to concentrate a selection of works, so that they represent one facet of the many trends now evident in today's art. The facet I have chosen is that of "technological art", which in simple terms, is the use of today's scientific discoveries – be they materials, relations or principles – to produce objects of art.

My art consultant, Dr. William Seitz, Director of Rose Museum at Brandeis University, and formerly Curator of Painting and Sculpture of the Museum of Modern Art of New York, and I have been engaged in a vigorous intellectual debate over the validity of the types of works that I insist upon collecting. This letter to you, therefore, is to request your assistance in aiding me to present to Dr. Seitz the arguments that I know you made to me and your other students concerning the function of art in its time, and its relationship to the science of its day. I don't recall whether I got these impressions from your lectures, or from one of your books, and I have reviewed without success almost all the books that you have had published – including the original text of the Philosophy of Science you used in your class (much of which is way beyond me today).

Please excuse the length of this letter, but I felt I should give you the background as fully as possible.

If it does not inconvenience you, the next time I am in New Haven I would like to take the opportunity to call upon you and say hello. In the meantime, I do hope that this letter finds you in the best of health.

Sincerely,
David W. Bermant (1940)
President
National Shopping Centers

THE GALLERY

PRIVATE COLLECTION

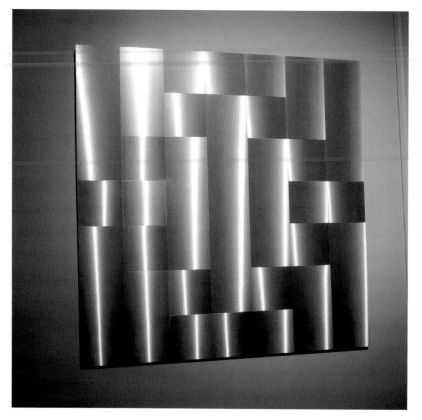

GETULIO ALVIANI
Superficie A Testura Vibratile
Opera Programmata 4019
1965
38"H x 38"W x 1"D

GETULIO ALVIANI

"This is the very first piece of art I ever bought anywhere. I purchased it in April 1965 from l'Obelisco Galleria in Rome. My two oldest children and my then wife and I were on a tour first of Israel, then of Rome, since the two civilizations were fairly similar in being antique, vibrantly current as well as religious. We walked into this gallery and the children spotted this piece on the wall in the middle of the show . . . and if I knew then what I know now, I'd have bought the whole show, but I didn't. And they said, 'Daddy, let's get that piece that looks like it weaves in and out.' Although it doesn't, it's an optical illusion. And when I found out the price, a thousand dollars, I said, 'Who pays $1000 for something like this?' Well, I guess I did. Because they convinced me we should have something as a memento of the trip. When I got back to New York I happened to go to the Museum of Modern Art and found that it had also purchased a piece by this same artist, and I thought my piece was far better. That shocked me a little."
—DWB

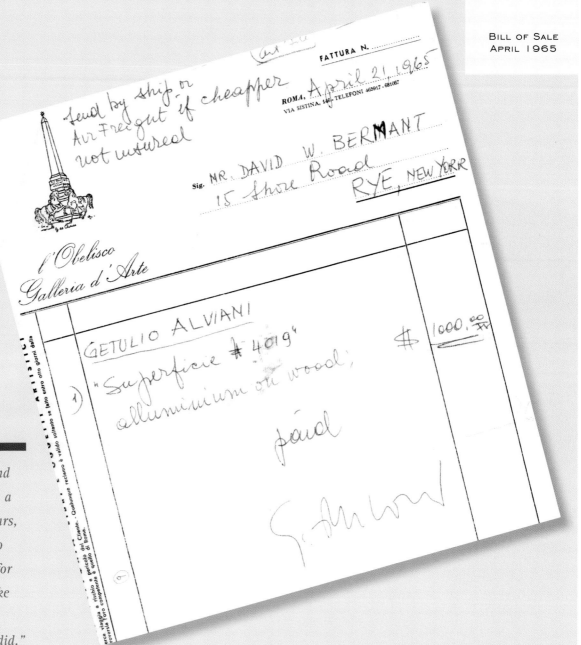

send by ship or
Air Freight if cheaper
not insured

FATTURA N. ....

ROMA, April 21, 1965
VIA SISTINA, 146 - TELEFONI 465917 - 681067

Sig. MR. DAVID W. BERMANT
15 Shore Road
RYE, NEW YORK

l'Obelisco
Galleria d'Arte

GETULIO ALVIANI

1) "Superficie # 4019"
alluminium on wood; $ 1000.00

paid

"When I found out the price, a thousand dollars, I said, 'Who pays $1000 for something like this?' Well, I guess I did."
—DWB

THE COLLECTION

"If you walk into the bedroom, you'll find a reclining woman, which is the title of the piece, dated 1970, by John de Andrea. This was acquired in 1970 through Ivan Karp's OK Harris Gallery in NYC. One of my favorite pieces—take one look at her, and you can see why."

JOHN DE ANDREA

Sculptor John de Andrea is associated with Hyperrealism and specializes in nudes. "Reclining Woman" is done in polyester resin, polychromed in oil with dynel. This life-sized nude was exhibited at the Whitney Museum, New York City, 1970 Bicentennial.

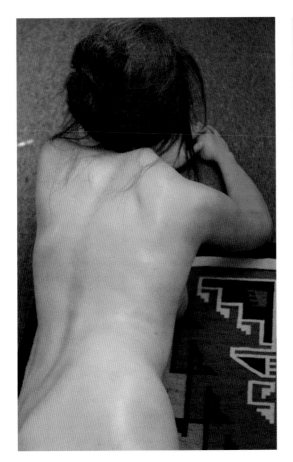

JOHN DE ANDREA
Reclining Woman
1970

*"When someone asked my first wife
whether 'Reclining Woman' moved,
my wife replied,
'When she moves, she goes.' "*
—DWB

I'm just after a really fine superstructure... I started to work from the nude because I've always liked classical sculpture, and I just kept going into superrealism. My people don't "do" very much because I try to keep as much interest as possible on their physical presence. I want to emphasize the beauty of the body.

John de Andrea
Born Denver 1941
U Col PFA 1965

THE COLLECTION

"This work was originally noisy, raw, and wild. David enjoyed that when this work was turned 'on' people jumped back with surprise. Later on, we made an update to that design and the work became quieter and less threatening."

—*Alejandro Siña*

ALEJANDRO SIÑA
Spinning Shaft
1978
67"H x 128"W x 37"D

ALEJANDRO & MOIRA SIÑA

ALEJANDRO & MOIRA SIÑA create kinetic lightworks that use electricity, glass, and luminous gases. Their work (much of it made for architectural and public spaces) requires viewer participation ranging from pressing a switch to clapping hands to simply touching an artwork to activate the light. Alejandro developed a new technique for using neon that eliminates bulky wiring apparatus and power supplies, which allows the neon to be put into motion. A native of Chile, Alejandro came to the United States on a Fulbright Scholarship in 1973 to continue his work as a Research Fellow at MIT's Center for Advanced Visual Studies. After the Fulbright grant, he was invited by MIT to continue as a Fellow, totaling six years at MIT. He and his wife Moira have worked as a team since 1978.

"The title of the piece is 'Spinning Shaft 1978,' and I don't hesitate to call it the best light piece I have ever seen. And I still think it's the best years after I bought it. I purchased it in 1983 from the artist, although it was made in '78. It consists of neon tubes and electric motor, but the results can hardly be summed up in that fashion. It was on display at every major space that borrowed pieces from my collection. It's just extraordinary."
—DWB

ALEJANDRO SIÑA
Spinning Shaft
1978
67"H x 128"W x 37"D

"David was very important in the direction of my work . . . I was able to continue to develop many Lightworks with his encouragement and funding, to bring ideas to reality. It was remarkable that I could explain to him by phone many concepts that he would approve for me to build. Many works were tricky to develop, and his patience was crucial in letting me have a chance to improve and revise my technology. The main quest was to make works that were reliable to operate, especially for outdoors. Many artists that worked with David benefited in developing their technology like I did. Many first working prototypes were commissioned by him in assorted technological media. He was very sharp with his comments, and you had to be very careful . . . It was not easy to deal with him, but also was lots of fun."

—*Alejandro Siña*

 "Never fails to elicit a 'WOW' from any viewer the slightest bit alive."

Opposite:
ALEJANDRO & MOIRA SIÑA
Lasso
1999
96"H x 36"D

Left:
ALEJANDRO SIÑA
Night Butterfly
1978
120"H x 72"W x72"D

THE COLLECTION

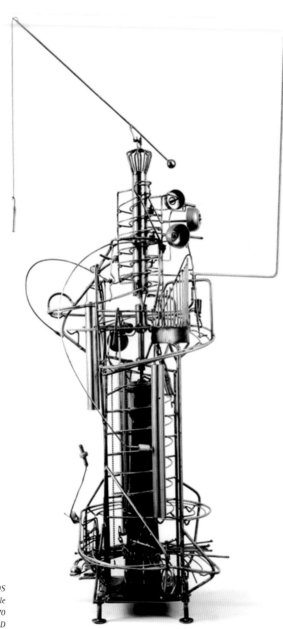

GEORGE RHOADS

"This is the very first piece I ever bought of George's. When George installed it in my home, I asked him whether it was the model for maybe a larger piece. He turned to me in surprise and said, 'Well yes, it could be. How did you know?' And I just said, 'I don't really know. What I'd like to see is a piece about five times bigger than this with several courses instead of just one . . . With different colors because I'd like to put it in a public space and I think the general public likes different colors.' He said, 'I can do that too.' I said, 'George, to do a piece that much bigger and more extensive, what do you think it would cost, and how long would it take?' He said, 'Probably cost $10,000 to $12,000 and would take probably six months.' Well two and a half years later and $25,000 later the piece was designed, created, and installed in the Long Ridge Mall in Rochester, New York. It's one of the very best pieces he's ever done and, not only that, pieces similar to it for other shopping centers cost $150,000. So I got a steal, right? I also took a chance, right? I did." —DWB

GEORGE RHOADS
Indestructible
1970
48"H x 10"W x 8"D

Opposite top left:
GEORGE RHOADS
Homage to Wolfgang
1981
25"H x 12"W x 12"D

Opposite bottom:
GEORGE RHOADS
Lunatick
1990
60"H x 36"W x 2"D

DWB

" 'Lunatick' consists of 112 clocks and batteries that are making all those lovely ticking sounds. You want to know who comes up with the titles? It's George Rhoads himself. Luna, for the moon that each one of these circles represent, and the tick, the ticking of the clocks."

George Rhoads in studio

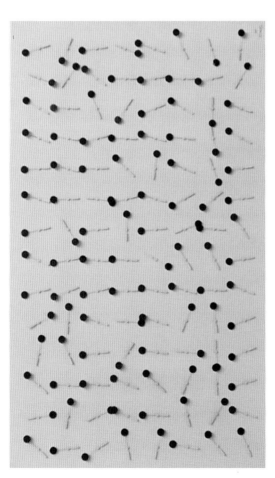

ORGANIZATION CHART
COUNTY OF SANTA BARBARA

The purpose of this display is to depict the organizational structure of Santa Barbara County. It differs from all other charts of its type in that it reflects reality, rather than theory.

In order to determine the working relationship between any two persons in the County organization, simply pick a dot (any one will do, they are faceless bureaucrats anyway). Then pick a second dot, representing the second person. Observe. You will notice that each bureaucrat runs around in its own little circle, with only incidental and accidental contact with any other. Congratulations! You now understand how things work around here.

A similar chart has been prepared for the Federal Government. It is the same in all respects except for its enormous size and the fact that the dots move at a pace undetectable to the human eye. (Author Unknown)

A clever interpretation of "Lunatick" written when it was on display in the Santa Barbara County Tax Office during the P.U.L.S.E. 2 exhibition in 1990

GEORGE RHOADS
Wallpiece #1
1981
31"H x 60"W x 8"D

"My income was pretty sporadic and David's commissions really helped . . . I really relied on David for my living for, I don't know, a few years."

—George Rhoads

"George called me up one day and said, 'Dave, I want to do a piece that you can either hang on a wall or put it on a shelf and it's gonna have a lot of little balls rolling back and forth, up and down, something like your "Indestructible I" yet completely different. All kinds of different things happening.'

"I said, 'How much will it cost?'

"He said, 'I have no idea.'

" 'How come?'

"He said, 'Well, I have to build one first and I've never built one, but I've just got a small section going, and I think you'd like it very much.'

"I said, 'Go ahead. It's fine with me.'

"So what we would do in those days is he would send me a figure for the materials so he could at least buy his materials, and then I paid him like a plumber. Ten or twelve dollars an hour, I think. And then George would go and build it and take as much time as it took. And they take a lot of time, believe me! And when he got through—and I trusted him implicitly, even though he may be working on hundred thousand dollar pieces now—and when he completed the piece it cost $5,289."

"I had Ivan Karp look at it, and when Ivan saw it he said, 'I want you to have George make a lot of these for me. These are the first works of art by George Rhoads that I think I can sell from the OK Harris Gallery.'

"So I became George's partner. I did all the financing, paid for all the materials, paid for his time, then he hired new people. We even did a few with Chris Hopmans, my curator.

"That's why I know what it takes to do and how long it takes to do them, because they're very intricate. But I must say, at the very end, Ivan was selling these individual wall pieces for $25,000 each. This is still #1. It's as good as any that he's done, although he has done some very, very beautiful ones, but this one is extremely beautiful."

DWB

THE COLLECTION

"What you have done and are doing I know at times is done against resistance, ignorance, and even common sense, but I believe it is so generous and so nurturing for all the people it touches, not just the artists, that it borders on the noble."

—Clyde Lynds

"I am anxious to get you started on building these new outdoor sculptures as soon as possible because I am convinced they will open a vast new area for you in the development of your work." (Letter to Clyde Lynds, November 1981)

DWB

CLYDE LYNDS
Rosetta Series, Moonstone I
1982
96"H x 45"W x 24"D

CLYDE LYNDS

Excerpts from correspondence between Clyde Lynds and DWB, December 6, 1981:

CLYDE RE: ROSETTA SERIES, "MOONSTONE I":

"The Rosetta Stone has always intrigued me as a wonderfully mysterious and suggestive object, and I wondered if a modern-day version of that could be built . . . it would relate to our world today, but also echo the past and the great mysterious monuments men have left behind."

DWB BACK TO CLYDE:

"I think your suggestion concerning the Rosetta Stone to be marvelous. I will be guided completely by your choice and taste, as I am confident I will end up with a most extraordinary thing done yet, and you know I think I have some extraordinary things within my purview. GO–GO–GO."

CLYDE BACK TO DWB:

"Mandalay, Cancun, Harrisburg, or Chicago–I'll go with you anywhere."

CLYDE LYNDS
Saturn's Other Moon
1973
8"H x 15"W x 10"D

"Clyde is one of my favorite artists starting way back in the 1970s. He is a master furniture maker as well as a master artist. His work is always magnificent. He's fighting the set ways of his time, those who refuse to recognize that art can be made of fiber optics. Nevertheless, he creates works of stunning beauty."

"Your energetic and total commitment to us and our work, David, has not only renewed our commitment to it, but given us hope that it will be seen in our lifetimes as work that is some of the most important being done today."

—Clyde Lynds, October 26, 1981

"I always come away from an evening in your presence hyped up, as if your energies and commitments were a contagious disease and I had fallen ill from it. I think if someone ever took a Kirlian photograph of your anatomy you'd short circuit the film."

—Clyde Lynds

Clyde Lynds & DWB

DWB

"In 1985, eleven years after the purchase of 'Spectral Wind,' I bought 'Cobalt Blue' directly from the artist. Price was the same, but no discount. This was a piece that Clyde designed based upon my urging him to design pieces that could go into public spaces, where you didn't have to turn out the lights completely in order to see the piece. Because you can't turn out the lights in a library or an airport or a shopping center. And so he did this and we had it in a shopping center, and it was reasonably successful. Not nearly as good as if it was completely dark, but at least good enough to see. And you can see the steps, or changes that Clyde made in his work over the eleven year period. This piece is much brighter, easier to see, and moves more quickly. When you go into a public space, I explained to Clyde, the general public comes through quickly, they're there for another reason, so they'll glance at your work. If you can hold their attention for a few minutes that's the best you can expect. I think this piece does that. Among other things, it seems to indicate that you're looking at a city from an airplane late at night. Others have other interpretations such as an airport. When I went over it with the artist, he just smiled and never did explain what he thought he was describing. If he had to do that he didn't have to make the piece, he insisted."

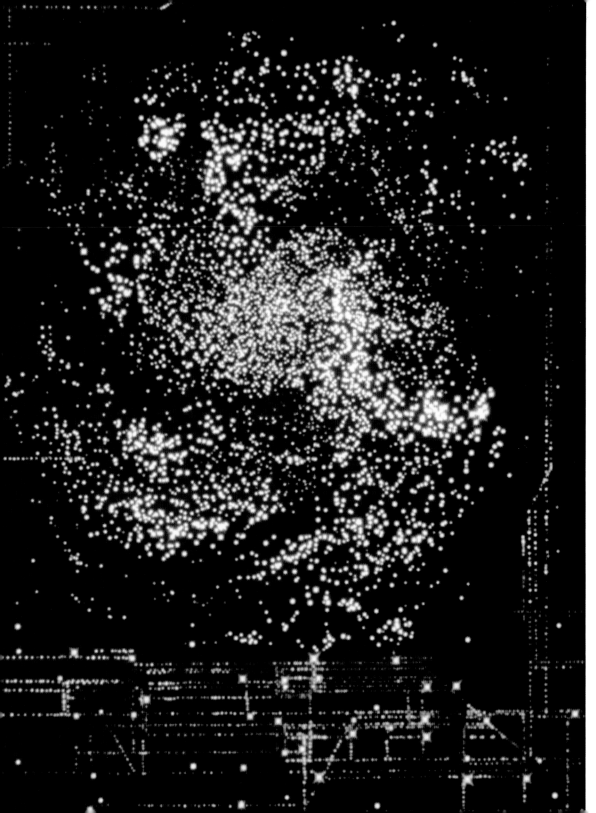

"An art without light
or movement falls
far short of touching
the reality of this
environment or even
the reality of nature.
Everything in nature
and in the cosmos is in
motion and in a state
of transformation.
The new reality is not
matter, but energy."

—Clyde Lynds

CLYDE LYNDS
Cobalt Blue
1985
78"H x 36"W x 12"D

THE COLLECTION

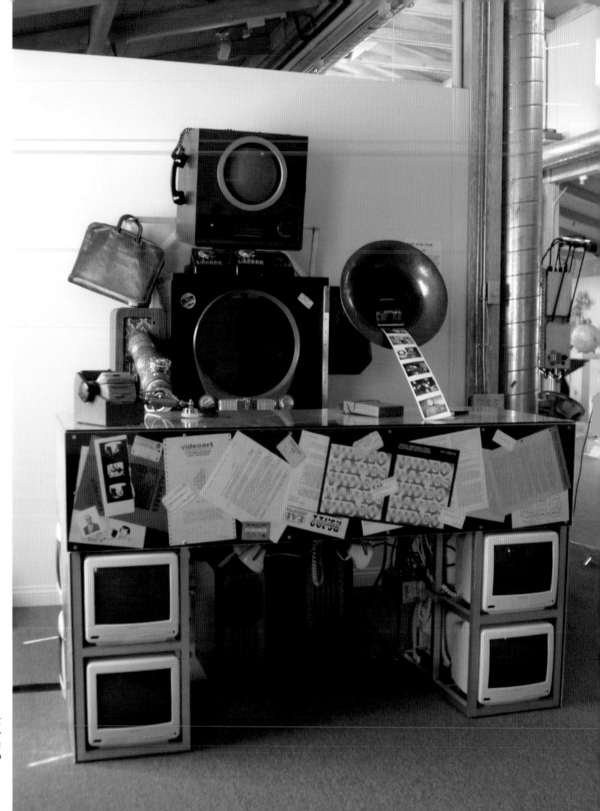

NAM JUNE PAIK
Virtually Wise
1994
82"H x 66"W x 66"D

NAM JUNE PAIK

"If you study the piece itself you will see why I hold it in such high regard. It's the form of a robot sitting at a desk, meaning Howard Wise's desk, and it contains many personal items from Howard, who besides being my art dealer was my personal friend. I'm proud to be listed under my National Shopping Center category in his Rolodex, along with many major artists of the day. You will see his credit cards, his money wallet, his file bag and many personal, intimate items. Among the more outrageous, reflecting Paik's sense of humor, is the reproduction of a memo that Howard had made in which he agreed to finance Paik's interest payments that he was unable to make on his Visa card, provided Paik did not make any more purchases. This was dated October 19, 1985, and then around the side of the piece and possibly faded by the sun, you'll see a check that apparently had been given to Paik by Barbara Wise, by mistake, a blank check which he filled out from Howard Wise to himself, Nam June Paik, a year later, in the amount of one million and thirty-four dollars. You don't see Howard's signature, however." –DWB

"Nam June Paik's 'Virtually Wise' is one of the master works of my collection . . . This piece is an intersecting of my slight career in the art world and Howard Wise's major career in the art world."
–DWB

DWB'S DESCRIPTION OF NAM JUNE PAIK AND "PARTICIPATION TV":

"Another piece similar to this was on display at the Howard Wise Gallery—one of the best galleries in the world for this form of art—in New York City in a show in 1969 called 'TV as a Creative Medium,' . . . and I paid $600 for the Paik piece, of which the artist probably got $300 to $400.

"I sent the piece to my shopping center in Rochester, New York, where we hung two microphones from the ceiling as well as the piece on the ceiling. We hung the microphones so that one was at an adult dimension and the other was at a child's dimension. A family going to the center could play with the Paik piece, as well as anyone else. It's a fairly simple piece, yet I like to have these pieces checked on by the artist from time to time. When I asked Paik to check on it when he went to Rochester, as I knew he did occasionally, he would always refuse. He never would tell me why. Finally one day, I found out he was mad I didn't pay enough money for the piece, as he thought $400 or whatever figure he used was not enough. You could never understand Paik in those days when he talked, except when he mentioned money, then you could understand him. So I said, 'What did I have to do with the price? I paid whatever price was on the piece. That's ridiculous.' But anyway, that was his reaction. And I used to ask him during those years to come up to my home and do a piece he talked about—a garden TV—and I said, 'I'd love to do that. Come on up.' I never discussed price or anything, just 'come up and do it,' and he never came.

"Finally, one year there was an exhibition called 'Soundings' at the Newburger Museum in Westchester County, where I lived. And there was this piece you're looking at. I called Paik up as soon as I saw it and said, 'Hey Paik. What's that piece doing in that show? You were only supposed to make one of these things, not two. Why don't you sell me that?' He said, 'Not for sale.' OK, not for sale, not for sale. 'All I'm going to do is put it in my personal collection.' 'Not for sale, David.'

"Two years later there was a grand retrospective given to Paik at the Whitney Museum. I went up to the opening along with James Wines, a good friend of mine who was also a close friend of Paik. As I approached the two of them, Paik turned to Wines and said, 'Here comes the guy who bought the first piece I ever sold in America, and the only piece I've ever sold in America.' This was twelve years later, and mind you I consider Paik the greatest artist in the world today—here is a man who only sold one piece in twelve years. Can you beat that?

"So once again I said to him, 'Paik, whose fault is that? After all I've asked you to come to my home. I never put a price on anything. Why haven't you ever shown up?' No answer. I said, 'Paik, why don't you sell me this piece for my personal collection?' 'Not for sale.' I got that same answer.

"A week or two later I was talking to Howard Wise and Howard had apparently partially financed the Paik show because his name was plastered all over the place. I said, 'Howard, tell me why that crazy artist of yours that I bought the piece from in 1969 won't sell me an identical second piece, also called "Participation TV." ' He said, 'He's on the other phone, David, I'll have him call you.' Sure enough Paik called me. Paik says, 'Howard say I should sell to you. You good guy.' I said, 'Sure I'm a good guy. How much do you want for it?' He said, 'I don't know.' I said, 'What do you mean, you don't know?!' He said, 'I don't know, David, I don't know how much money I want for piece.' I said, 'Think a minute. You must have some idea what your art's worth.' Silence. Then all of a sudden I hear him say, 'I got idea, David. I tell you what, I owe lots of money for this show. I owe men I hire, I owe for pieces of material I have to buy . . . lots of money. I tell you what, you pick up all bills, the piece is yours.' I said, 'Well do you have any idea how much you spent?' He said, 'No.' I thought a minute and said, 'You made a deal. Send the bills.' So he did. I get a bill for $400 here, $200 there, $900 here, $600 there, $80, $40, $50 . . . and after about three months the bills stop coming and I get a short note from Paik, 'All bills paid. Piece is yours.' You want to know what I paid? I ain't gonna tell you. But a fraction of what I would have paid if I'd bought the piece through a gallery, because I've since had it appraised."

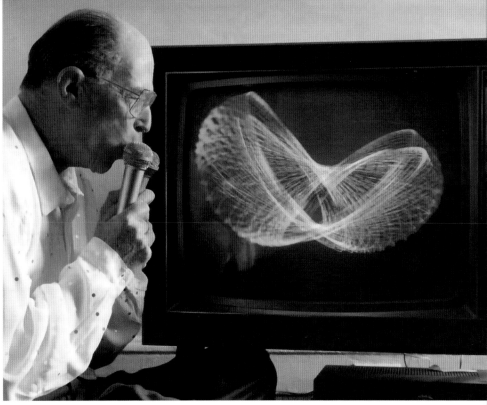

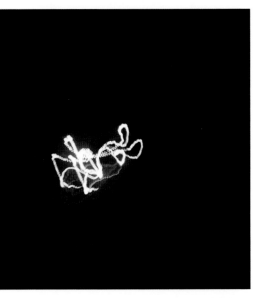

NAM JUNE PAIK

NAM JUNE PAIK
Participation TV
1969
30"H x 32"W x 24"D

Nam June Paik, considered by many to be the father of video art, was born in Seoul, Korea in 1932. He was the first artist employing modern technology to be given a retrospective exhibition at the Whitney Museum, New York. An original member of the Fluxus group centered in Europe during the 1960s, he had exhibitions in most of the important museums of the world.

DWB

"One of my very favorite pieces—this was done by Nam June Paik, pronounce it "PAKE," he prefers that. If you hear me slip every now and then, you'll know it's my age. Nam June called it 'Participation TV 1969.'"

THE COLLECTION

"My work is really Mother Nature's jewelry. I'm pretty sure one of Dave's mistresses was Mother Nature."

—James Ossi

JAMES OSSI
Bubble Sculpture
1980
96"H x 57"W x 20"D

"I make machines that blow everlasting, upward moving, iridescent, huge, square soap bubbles. Oddly, I viewed these contraptions as science, not art. I thought MIT might be interested, so I approached the Institute a few days after meeting Dave for the first time. MIT asked, 'How much?' I answered, 'Thirty thousand dollars.' They said, 'Can you get matching funds?' I asked Dave, and immediately he said, 'Sure.' He gave fifteen thousand. That was in 1980. MIT has had one of my sculptures in the lobby of their physics building ever since."

—James Ossi

JAMES OSSI

James Ossi, born in 1947 in Wyckoff, New Jersey, graduated from the Parsons School of Design. While working in its research department, he created his first bubble sculptures. The bubble machine constructions were displayed in the fall of 1981 at the OK Harris Gallery in New York and have been seen on "Ripley's Believe It or Not!" TV program.

DWB

"[The Bubble Sculpture] is one of my very favorite pieces, and I kind of hide it away from everybody. It used to be in my sunroom in Rye overlooking water, a very glorious location. But we captured some of its glory by putting it here against the hill, which we've filled with some cacti. When it goes on, it's magnificent."

JAMES OSSI'S REFLECTIONS ON DWB:

At the mention of the name, Dave Bermant, a thousand contradictory memories and messages flash and argue and laugh and digress. There is no escaping the inner conflict that arises just by hearing the name, Dave Bermant.

My earliest memory of Dave: I had a few photos of square, iridescent soap bubbles, and I drove through the gates of his stone and brick castle on the edge of Long Island Sound, on the cusp of New York City, on the Westchester Riviera, next door to the famous Zealot-And-Blow-Hard, Reverend Ike—and down the street from Playland's noisy kiddy rides and the famous, ancient Dragon roller coaster.

I was there because an hour earlier I had just met Ivan Karp, who was, to my mind, Chairman Of The Board Of Art Gallery Gods And Smokers Of Expensive Cigars. He glanced at my photos and simply said, "Go." He slipped the address in my hand and added, "I'll call. Go now."

The stone columns seemed like they were a thousand feet in front of the Castle. The columns were massive and menacing, as the former owner's architect demanded. However, their vulgar phallic hostility was circumvented and turned into a kind of laughing post because their present owner, Dave Bermant, topped each ten-foot-high stone column with a stroboscopic, wonderful, whimsical, whirling, swooping luminescence of some giant fantastical insect from a galaxy far away.

I parked under the grandfather elms and near a large, sparkling Japanese kimono. The material for this kimono wasn't featherweight silk, but four tons of concrete—a gravestone of sorts. The sparkles in the monument were fiber optics imbedded in the concrete and moved rhythmically, spelling out words in strange tongue and alphabet from that other galaxy.

I took my photos up the flagstone walk to the Castle

entry. I passed through a garden of waist high, square, metal flowers whose thousand lights moved rhythmically. Curiosity forced me to touch a bloom. The plant quivered, sucked the mechanical bloom into its stalk and disappeared down under the flowerbed. Gone. Other mechanical flowers followed like lemmings. The robotic flowers were not shy, they were chicken.

The large mirror to the right of the Castle entry inverted my image, not only top to bottom, not only left to right, but inside out—my nose looked like it was in back of my head, behind my face. My reflected imagery was tiny and made me feel puny and upside-down and all inverted. I stood there in this Twilight Zone. It was a zone not of fear, but of comical chicanery. I was in an otherworldly location—yet one so close to the City.

"Stick your head in the mirror," said The Voice. I looked around but saw no one. I didn't know what to do. "Stick your head in the mirror," said The Voice.

I moved my face toward the middle of the large, round mirror. Sure enough, it seemed to open, and I could advance my face beyond the perimeter and into a kind of chromium cave. I blinked. The reflection of my face was now reversed, no longer upside down or inside out. More impressively, I was huge. My head looked spherical and ten feet in diameter.

"Okay, you mensch! You passed the test!" said The Voice. "The draw bridge is lowered. You may enter through the wooden door to the left. Welcome to my world."

The man who whipped open the medieval door was thin like Mahatma Gandhi and naked like Mahatma Gandhi and had a wide smile like the Mad Hatter in Alice in Wonderland. Behind him, in the Castle, were flashes of mechanical spirits and sundry miracles of joy.

Q & A WITH JAMES OSSI:

Q: What do you think it was about your art that brought David so much pleasure?

A: My work is really Mother Nature's jewelry. I'm pretty sure one of Dave's mistresses was Mother Nature.

Q: What did you most appreciate about David?

A: His joy. He brought it everywhere and spread it around freely.

Q: What do you think was David's greatest strength?

A: Again: His joy. And his jokes and drive to spread joy to all. He was one of the Great Gods of Joy. I'm a lucky guy to have known him.

"David had fabulous birthday parties on the vast acreage behind the Castle. These parties were always well populated by lots and lots of colorful artists. Some were wacky, some actually thought they were profound—these were the really insane ones."

—James Ossi

JAMES SEAWRIGHT
Orbits V
1998
46"H x 19"W x 19"D

JAMES SEAWRIGHT

DWB once referred to James Seawright as "the best electronic artist in the world." Born in 1936 in Jackson, Mississippi, James Seawright served in the US Navy before moving to New York City in 1961. He began teaching at Princeton University in 1969 and served as the Director of Visual Arts at Princeton from 1975 to 2001. Seawright retired from Princeton in 2009.

A pioneer in kinetic, electronic sculpture, Seawright usually builds only electronic pieces. An exception is "Mirror XVII," which he created in 1987 as an interactive public piece that was well received in DWB's shopping centers.

> "For David to be so supportive was awe-inspiring for us, I think, and so it was a two-way street.
> It really was a pleasure to know David, and the fact that he cared about our work was a plus.
> It was something extra thrown in."
>
> —James Seawright

Above and left:
JAMES SEAWRIGHT
Mirror XVII
1987
72"H x 72"W x 4"D

JAMES SEAWRIGHT'S REFLECTIONS ON DWB:

David would tell people on the slightest excuse that when he was at Yale one of the most influential professors was a man named F.S.C. Northrop. I believe he's a philosopher, but he put the idea in David's head that the art of a given time should be the art that deals with the technology of that time. And he would argue that that's exactly the way it was with the Greeks and the Romans and the Renaissance; people like Leonardo, they were really leading technologists, and at the same time they were principal artists. And his whole spiel was that he wanted to collect that kind of art because he felt it was the most significant, and he wanted to put it in public places because that's what the Greeks did. So he saw my work as falling into that category precisely, that it was dealing with modern technology, and yet it was something that was not surrounded by a lot of hocus-pocus, but was something that could be popular, could be actually appreciated by people without a lot of theoretical baggage.

"It consists of 144 mirrors. If you walk to a certain spot not too far from the piece, if you look into it, you'll see yourself 144 times—if you can stand it, it's an interesting piece."

—DWB

"This is one of the outstanding creations of my collection and it has stood the test of time. While it occasionally has mechanical glitches its beauty nevertheless remains outstanding. And the glitches somehow or other are always solved. The way the machine opens and shuts is interesting, but to my mind the real creativity and beauty comes from the various combinations of colors and movement that the artist has created. The diodes change colors very quickly or slowly as the artist has programmed the computer. It's a stunning display."
—DWB

JAMES SEAWRIGHT
House Plants
1984

"David was always pushing us in directions we didn't necessarily want to go."

—James Seawright

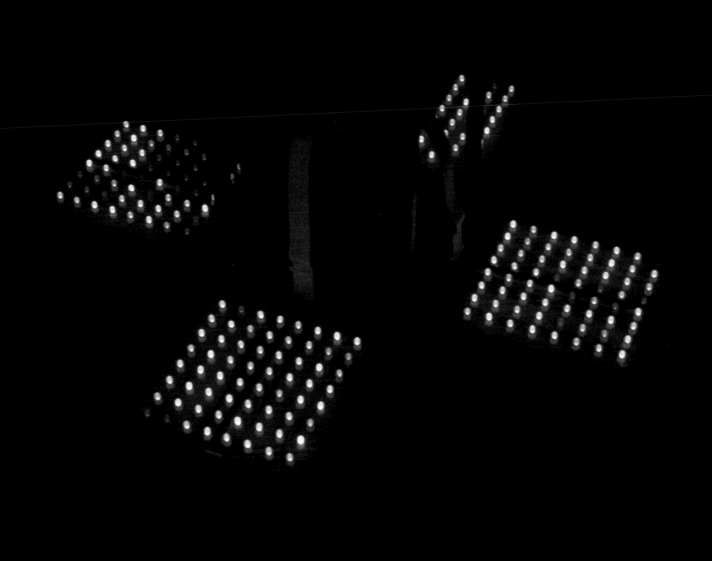

MARCEL DUCHAMP
Rotorelief
1935–1953 (115/150)
Frame, 14" square;
Set of 6 discs, 8" diameter

MARCEL DUCHAMP

"In early 1977, it was suggested to DWB that the acquisition of a Rotorelief with motor by Marcel Duchamp would be a worthy addition to the home collection as it establishes a historical reference to the kinds of work that make up the collection. After all, Duchamp was the first one who demonstrated that art need not be confined to paints and canvas.

"The Rotorelief, while an edition, was the most reasonable type purchase, considering the asking prices of his ready-mades and the unavailability of most of his work. It would demonstrate both the optical and movement phases incorporated in the private collection.

"A simple signed set that can be properly displayed over the mantle piece in the living room was what DWB wanted to obtain.

"In May 1979, after speaking with several people who were knowledgeable about Marcel Duchamp and his work, DWB purchased Rotorelief disks and motorized machine from Paul Shanley, publisher of 'Art in America.' " –DWB

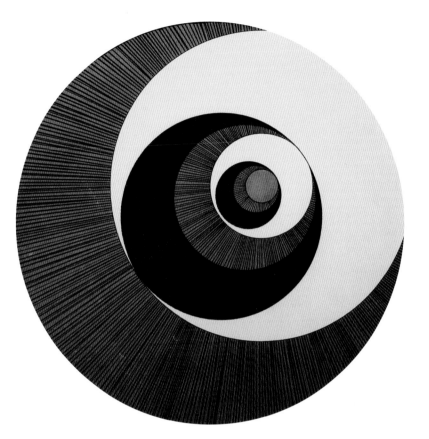

> *"My present wife, Susan Hopmans, is a graduate of Hunter College and maintains that Duchamp is the most influential artist of the 20th century. Naturally, I agree."*
> —DWB

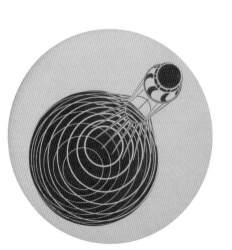

THE COLLECTION

*"Milton Komisar
has elected to join
us, so that makes
one more light
artist. Those of you
who know his work
will welcome him;
those of you who
don't should get to
know it."
—DWB*

MILTON KOMISAR
Little Bang
1991

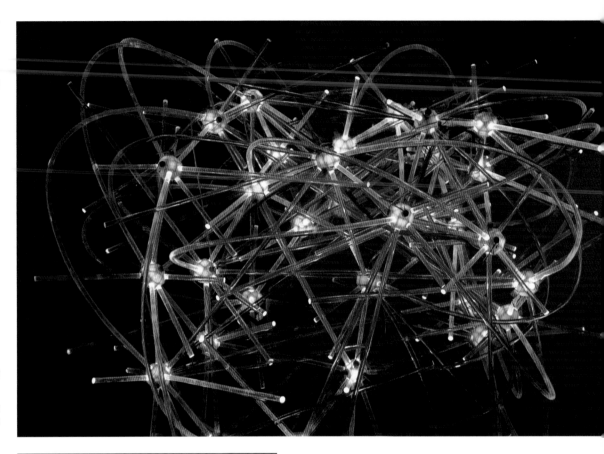

MILTON KOMISAR

"This piece by Milton Komisar is called 'Little Bang,' done in 1991. It's 4' x 5' and 52" high. We saw it on display at the Center for the Arts at Yerba Buena Gardens in San Francisco in 1994 and acquired it for our collection. Milton's sculptures have a beauty all their own . . . reflective, meditative. This one is just delightful." —DWB

"My favorite aspect of the whole relationship I had with David Bermant was that at a certain period in my life I needed someone to come in and say, 'I support what you do, and I'll pay you for it. I'll give you a venue for your work. I will take you out of the pure subjectivity of being an artist cooped up in a studio making stuff that nobody wants.' "

—Milton Komisar

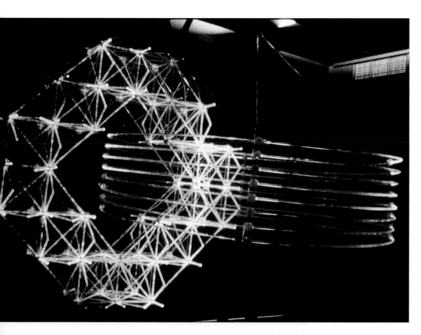

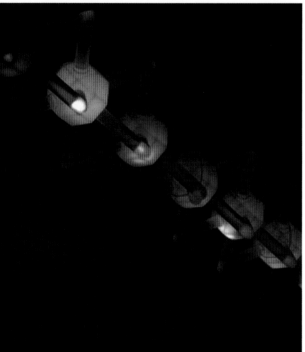

Above:
MILTON KOMISAR
Rhapsody on a Theme
by F. Scott Key
1987
72"H x 72"W x 12"D

Left:
MILTON KOMISAR
Get Your Ducks All in
a Row
1996
Santa Barbara Public
Library

MILTON KOMISAR'S REFLECTIONS ON DWB:

The thing about David was he was a very generous person as long as he could be active in the generosity. And that's the way he was with all of the artists he supported. He didn't just buy their work and then put it in some big room or gallery in his house or something. That was part of it.

But the other part was—I mean that was important, but the personal connection that he had with a lot of the artists whose work he bought was really important to him—it was his way of being involved, and being a part of the ages, in the '70s, '80s, '90s.

He took his wealth and he spent it so that he could participate in the culture that at the time was just beginning—which was the culture as it related to technology and the use of the technology—and then to take the step of taking the technology and bringing it into art. He took his wealth and it made it possible for him to participate in that.

I don't know who else was so committed to that, but he was really emotionally committed to it. He responded from his gut.

Psychologically, emotionally, conceptually, he sensed that the use of technology in art was important, and he wanted to be a part of it. So he took his money and he found artists and he bought their work. And because of the nature of his personality—he was rough and tumble; he was a New York Jew—so he had a lot of rough edges to him and he annoyed a lot of people, and he was irrational and kind of bossy. But his instincts were good. And he was able to be giving and supportive of a lot of artists, and I'm one of 'em.

Some people sort of gave him credit for what he did, but the art world in general didn't accept him because he didn't wear the right suit. The art world is really the worst place in the world to be. I have a lot of negative feelings about that whole reality. But at any rate, he never got the proper respect from the art world.

I think David liked to be hypnotized by the art. I mean I think that's why he liked my light sculptures because he would look at them, and the colors would go on and off and flip around and whatever, and light can be very hypnotic.

You couldn't argue with him. If you argued with him, he'd just get mad at you. He took everything very personally. He would think he was being objective and rational 'cause he was a businessman and well-educated. But he really lived in his feelings.

STEPHEN GERBERICH

From a pack rat's treasure trove of motors, toys, and other bric-a-brac, Iowa-born sculptor Stephen Gerberich builds some of the most entertaining contraptions you've ever seen. An alchemist of odds and ends, he's always searching for possibilities: a plastic dinosaur for this, a lampshade for that. He spins them all together in an elaborate call and response; call it a dialogue between mechanical memories and active imagination. Some of his myriad influences are Cornell, Rauschenberg, Duchamp, Tinguely, Kienholz, and especially his late brother, Tim.

A self-proclaimed lover of hand tools or any useful invention without a power cord, Gerberich turns discarded labor-saving devices into a wealth of fantastical sculptures. Push a button or spin a crank and these marvels come alive: buzzing, whirring, squeaking, humming, clanking, chugging, flashing, and blinking.

"In 1999, David Bermant honored me with his final commission, to build a sculpture at his ranch. For the western setting, I conceived of 'Yo Jimbo' from the title of a Kurosawa film. 'Yojimbo' means bodyguard in Japanese, and describes qualities I associate with Bermant: resilience and guardianship."

—Stephen Gerberich

STEPHEN GERBERICH
Yo Jimbo in studio
1994

Left:
STEPHEN GERBERICH
Yo Jimbo & Sonny
1999

Above:
DWB in Stephen Gerberich's studio

"David did love these artists, and he did love the art. Where his art is now, he's in that area, watching people come in and look at his art. I'm positive of it."

—*Bob Bermant, December 2008*

THE COLLECTION

"Your philosophy to share these whimsical or more profound delights with the largest number of people is very much akin to what a museum should do. One should not be afraid of art or the creativity of the artist!"

—Paul Perrot, Director, Santa Barbara Museum of Art

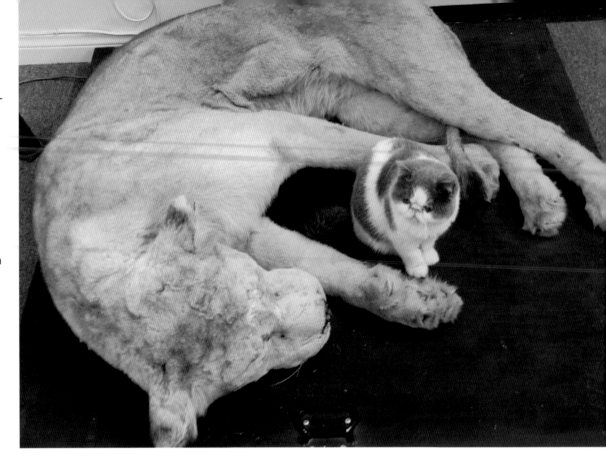

"There's breathing sounds by the lioness that you have to have the curator turn on for you, both the breathing sounds and movement, to hear and see the lion. The breathing sounds were produced by DWB, because I once went to the Bronx Zoo with a microphone and asked him to record the sounds of his breathing lions, and the curator there thought I was crazy. And he said, 'Why don't you just do it yourself? You can mimic the motions of the lion.' Which is what I did, because the lion's artist couldn't make it work so that there was a synchronization between the movement and the sounds naturally."

DWB

GUNTER WESELER

"Dreamers of Decadence" was purchased in June 1978 from the Electric Gallery in Toronto, Canada. When bringing the lioness from Canada into the United States the art piece was seized by U.S. Customs as a violation of the Endangered Species Act. After proving it was an African lioness, not an Indian lioness—and therefore not an endangered species—and that she was born, lived and died in a zoo in Amsterdam, the piece was released by Customs.

UNITED STATES
DEPARTMENT OF THE INTERIOR
FISH AND WILDLIFE SERVICE
FEDERAL BUILDING, ROOM 1114
111 WEST HURON STREET
BUFFALO, NY 14202
(716) 846-5661

CERTIFIED MAIL

Mr. David Bermant
15 Shore Road
Rye, New York 10580

Date July 6, 1978

Dear Sir:

You are hereby notified that the undersigned has detained one (1) female
Lion   *shipped to you in foreign commerce by* The Electri
Gallery, 24 Hazelton Avenue, Toronto Canada

Your shipment was detained at U.S. Customs Peace Bridge, Buffalo, N.Y.
on 07/03/78 *for the reason(s):*

_____ *that a Declaration for Importation of Fish or Wildlife, Form 3-177,
(enclosed) has to be filed with the U.S. Fish and Wildlife Service or the
District Director of Customs at the New York port where clearance under
50 CFR 14.52 occurs.*

__X__ *that the article(s) detained contain parts or products of a species
of wildlife classified in an Appendix of the Convention on International
Trade in Endangered Species. The importation of these articles requires
documentation (described in Sections 23.12 and 23.14 of Part 50 Code of
Federal Regulations) pertaining to the legality of export from the country
of origin.*

*If no response is received from this notice within 30 days, the parcel
will be seized and the Fish and Wildlife Service will initiate civil
proceedings for forfeiture for violation of the Endangered Species Act,
16 USC 1538(e).*

Sincerely yours,

Rodney C. Hanlon
Rodney C. Hanlon
Special Agent

RCH:cfd
Enclosures (Indicated):
( ) *Form 3-177*
( ) *Endangered Species Act of 1973*
(X) *50 CFR Part 14*
(X) *50 CFR Part 17*
(X) *50 CFR Part 23*

*"This was shown
at the Wadsworth
Atheneum in their
Lyon's Gallery . . .
Hear that? Lyon's
Gallery. Also at the
Alternative Museum
in New York City
in 1987, for a
show there. So yes,
Johnny, it is art."
—DWB*

DAVID W. BERMANT
150 PURCHASE STREET
RYE, NEW YORK 10580

CERTIFIED MAIL   July 10, 1978
RETURN RECEIPT

Mr. Rodney C. Hanlon
Special Agent
U. S. Fish & Wildlife Service
Federal Building — Room 1114
111 West Huron Street
Buffalo, New York 14202

Dear Mr. Hanlon:

In response to your form letter of July 6, 1978, I wish to advise you that information as requested by the various articles of the Code of Federal Regulations you forwarded me are in the process of being supplied to you as quickly as possible.

I tried reading the Regulations over the weekend but I must confess that I really would have to hire a Philadelphia lawyer to interpret them for me as I am convinced they were drawn up by one if not two of them. I think this is what President Carter has been referring to in his attempts (frustrated thus far) to have the bureaucratic language rewritten.

Although I am a university graduate, and have not ignored continuing my education since my graduation almost 40 years ago, I find the Regulations impossible to read with certainty. Would you be good enough, apart from your official capacity, to inform me in simple language exactly what is needed by your department to release my art object?

Incidentally, the Asiatic lion is the only one I found on the endangered list that you sent me and I have been advised that not only is my lioness of African vintage, but that it was bred, born and died in a captive environment in said area.

I do hope to have documentation concerning the above reach your hands in due order.

Many thanks for your cooperation.

Sincerely,

David W. Bermant

David W. Bermant

"It was a pleasure to see the wonderful works of art that Mr. Bermant acquired during his lifetime. It is truly an amazing group of objects, each with its own unique place within the history of the collection."

—Julie Joyce, Curator of Contemporary Art, Santa Barbara Museum of Art

SALLY WEBER

Sally Weber is an exceptional artist who works with the color and movement of light through time. Her art integrates holographic materials into architectural spaces and their environment. She holds a Master of Science in Visual Studies from MIT. Weber produces public installations and has exhibited widely throughout the United States and abroad.

"I am honored to have one of my works included in your collection. which is a singularly unique and inspiring one. I have always felt that 'Threshold of a Singularity' is one of my strongest installations."

—Sally Weber to DWB, February 1998

SALLY WEBER
Threshold of a Singularity—A Memorial
1989

"Sally Weber is an artist I met fifteen years ago when she was a student at MIT in their Center for Advanced Visual Studies program. Otto Piene, the director, invited me to give a talk to a class about my art collecting. At the end of my talk, she came up to me and said she'd like me to see a piece she had done. So, I went with her and I saw a beautiful piece made out of holograms. I said, 'You're for me.' "

"This installation marks the transition between reason and imagination where light, time and space fuse. In memory of my father."

—Sally Weber

THE COLLECTION

BASCHET BROTHERS
Musical Fountain
1974
58"H x 38"W

"The president of the University of California at Santa Barbara came to my home one night for dinner. And when she saw this piece, she said, 'Mr. Bermant, I have to have this in my home on the campus. Please lend it to me.' So I loaned it to her, and she kept it for three years. When she finally left, I got back my piece. I won't do that again. But I know she enjoyed it. She put it in her garden right at the entrance to her home. It's a very lovely piece."

DWB

BASCHET BROTHERS

French-born brothers Francois and Bernard Baschet are inventors and kinetic artists of sound sculptures and musical instruments. Francois, a sculptor, and Bernard, an engineer, have collaborated on their creations since 1952. Their sculptures are formed using stainless steel or aluminum and often interact with either wind or water.

N 912 DAX (Landes) 40
Les Bains de boue Hommes
Photo prise à l'Hôtel du Palais

Dear David,
    I am finishing the wind-
mills and am planning to
fly to NYC with them in my
suitcase to save time and
custom problems.
    I'll try to be there
about Oct.20th.
    Anyway, I'll call you as
sonn as I'll be in the US.
    No news from the pumps
but one of the aims of my
trip is to get them, alive
or dead.
    Let us greet each other
as we are great people.

F Baschet

Mr David Bermant
National Shopping Centers
150 Purchase Street
RYE
New York
10580
USA

PARIS 05
13H30
-8-
197

RÉPUBLIQUE FRANÇAISE

*Postcard from
Francois Baschet to DWB*

"The things I appreciated most about
David were his good taste, his optimism,
his energy when he made a decision,
and his humanity. I think his greatest
strength was his energy, his tenacity
when his decision was made."

—*Francois Baschet*

*BASCHET BROTHERS
Musical Roses
1973*

THE COLLECTION

OTTO PIENE
Light Ballet
1970
16"H x 29" diameter

OTTO PIENE

In 1957, Otto Piene cofounded the German artist group ZERO with Heinz Mack. At the time Piene created "Light Ballet" he was Director of the MIT Center for Advanced Visual Studies, an organization that was founded to encourage collaboration between artists and engineers. "Light Ballet" is a metal drum with rotating lights that was commissioned by DWB through the Howard Wise Gallery in 1970 after he saw a similar piece in the home of Howard Wise. When the piece is turned on, the light "ballerina" dances around the room. For many years "Light Ballet" was used as a coffee table in DWB's home in New York.

Comments by visitors to DWB's private collection:

"The sights and sounds of the incredible tour of David's collection have stayed with me this past week, resonating and opening new pathways in my brain."

—*Gallery visitor*

"Your passion for this art makes it come alive, even without the added elements of movement and surprise."

—*Gallery visitor to DWB*

THE COLLECTION

MATTIE BERHANG
Moet
1980
68"H x 72"W x 14"D

MATTIE BERHANG

DWB

"This piece was specially designed for our hall entrance in Rye, New York. As you can see it is quite delightful. It's a mobile, except we don't have any wind for it. It's a collection, as Ivan Karp once said, that comes from the leftovers of an industrial society. That's as good a description as any. I used to be a jogger and Mattie put a little jogger in there, and I certainly drink champagne, or I did in those days, and that's where the Moet comes from. There are other details of an intimate nature that are scattered throughout the piece. It's quite intriguing."

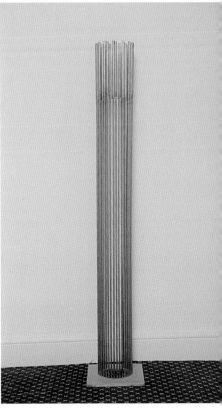

HARRY BERTOIA
Wind Chimes, Cathedral Series
1972
57"H x 10"W x 10"D

HARRY BERTOIA

"Harry Bertoia was a furniture designer as well as a superb sound artist, and there are two pieces in my collection that show his work. I bought them in 1973 from the Staempfli Gallery. One is eight feet high with two rods, and I had that one in my office. I used it to call my secretary . . . I want to tell you when that thing hit, she came running! I loaned one of them to a museum for an exhibition, and they put it in a fenced off area. I approached the piece, ready to climb onto the platform to demonstrate what the piece is supposed to do when you interact with it. A guard stopped me and said, 'Don't you dare touch that piece!' I said, 'But that's the only way you know what the piece is . . . it makes sound.' He said, 'I don't care what it makes. Don't you dare touch it!' I said, 'I own the piece. I ought to know what the heck I'm doing.' He says, 'I don't care . . . you own it . . . you don't own it . . . stay away from the piece!' " –DWB

THE COLLECTION

DUSTIN SHULER
Skinned Telephone
1986

DUSTIN SHULER

By Justin DiPego

DWB first saw Dustin Shuler's works at the Alternative Museum in New York, and he was interested. He gave Shuler his address in Santa Barbara and told him to send over some slides. Back in California, Shuler did just that. DWB called. He wanted to visit the studio. Shuler didn't have a studio, he had a work shop. Down came DWB, from Santa Barbara to Inglewood. Around the back and down the alley, he knocked on the door of the shop.

When Bermant stepped in with his wife, Susan, at his side, he saw a piece on the wall and immediately asked, "How much is that?"

"$500," said Shuler.

"Sold," said Bermant.

It was a skinned telephone, cut up and laid flat and framed with the handset hanging down from a long cord. Now that's an auspicious way to start, thought Shuler. He would come to see more of that in his long association with Bermant. The collector was direct, he knew what he liked, he knew what he wanted, and he knew what he'd pay for it.

Later on, Shuler knew DWB as a mentor, a father figure. When an art consultant wanted to borrow a piece of Shuler's to display in a business lobby, he was ready to go ahead with the loan. But DWB already owned the piece and he had one condition: the consultant had to pay rent. Why should she get something for nothing? And she didn't have to pay DWB, the owner, she had to pay Shuler, the artist.

Artists are regularly taken advantage of in situations like this. With DWB's encouragement, Shuler insisted on the rental fee and he got it. The consultant, however, never

DUSTIN SHULER
Albatross V
1995
18"H x 156"W x 80"D
(on 20' pole)

called him again. "Kid," said DWB, "I don't know if I'm helping you or hurting you."

"Dave was very generous," Shuler would later say, "but he wasn't stupid. He wouldn't over pay and I didn't over charge. So, it worked out."

Money is always a factor but so is inspiration. DWB was not an artist, but he was inspired. So, he'd go to his artists and he'd lay out an idea. He'd listen to a proposal or look at a model or a sketch, and if he didn't like it he was not afraid to say, "No." But more important, he was also not afraid to say, "What else you got?" And it was that sprit of, "what else you got?" that ever moved him forward.

"Listen kid," DWB said to Shuler, "I'm doing this thing where I've got this twenty-foot tall pole, and I want sculptures on top of it that move with the wind or do something . . . What do you got?"

A bit of back and forth and Shuler came up with the "Albatross." Actually, "Albatrosses" because there were seven of them. Atop the twenty-foot pole floats a sculpture shaped like a sailplane. With a wingspan of thirteen feet, it matches the great wandering albatrosses of the South Seas. Turning in the wind, the "Albatross" reflects the sun off its 24-karat gold skin.

Five Albatrosses belonged to DWB; three were in shopping centers; one stands at the Santa Barbara Airport; one at DWB's home. But perhaps more important than that support, from patron to artist, when Shuler sold "Albatross VI" to a museum in Wichita, Kansas, DWB was the first person he called. "I knew he would be happy," said Shuler. And that was the key to the relationship. DWB wanted his artists to do well. "Because of him, I sold a major piece and it helped me a lot."

David Bermant called Dustin Shuler, "one of the great artists of my time." And when DWB wondered if his no nonsense, straight forward methods were a help or a hindrance to the artist, Shuler replied, "You don't owe me anything. You've allowed me to do some of my greatest work."

In May 2010, Dustin Shuler set aside his last piece of work, clearing his list of things to do. He passed away at the age of sixty-two.

THE COLLECTION   BARNEY TOBEY

"Starting at the left, Marini, David Smith, Giacometti, Stankiewicz, Calder, Nevelson, and, good Lord, my wife and Harvey Peterson!"

September 22, 1976

Mr. B. Tobey
NEW YORKER MAGAZINE
25 West 43rd. Street
New York, New York

PLEASE FORWARD

Dear Mr. Tobey:

Ever since your delightful cartoon concerning the art
collector showing his collection, including the final kinetic one of
his wife in action, appeared in the New Yorker I have been the recipient
of many copies from various well meaning friends,as I have an art
collection consisting mostly of technological objects which move.

Inasmuch as the final subject of your cartoon is very much
akin to kinetic action and would thus be most appropriate to my collection
I was wondering if you would consider, if you haven't already done so,
selling your original cartoon to me?

Sincerely, yours,

David W. Bermant

DWB:bcb

PS: If you have any interest in viewing kinetic and technological art
a tour of the collection and a delightful meal with reasonably good
wines would be a part of the quid pro quo (as well as money).

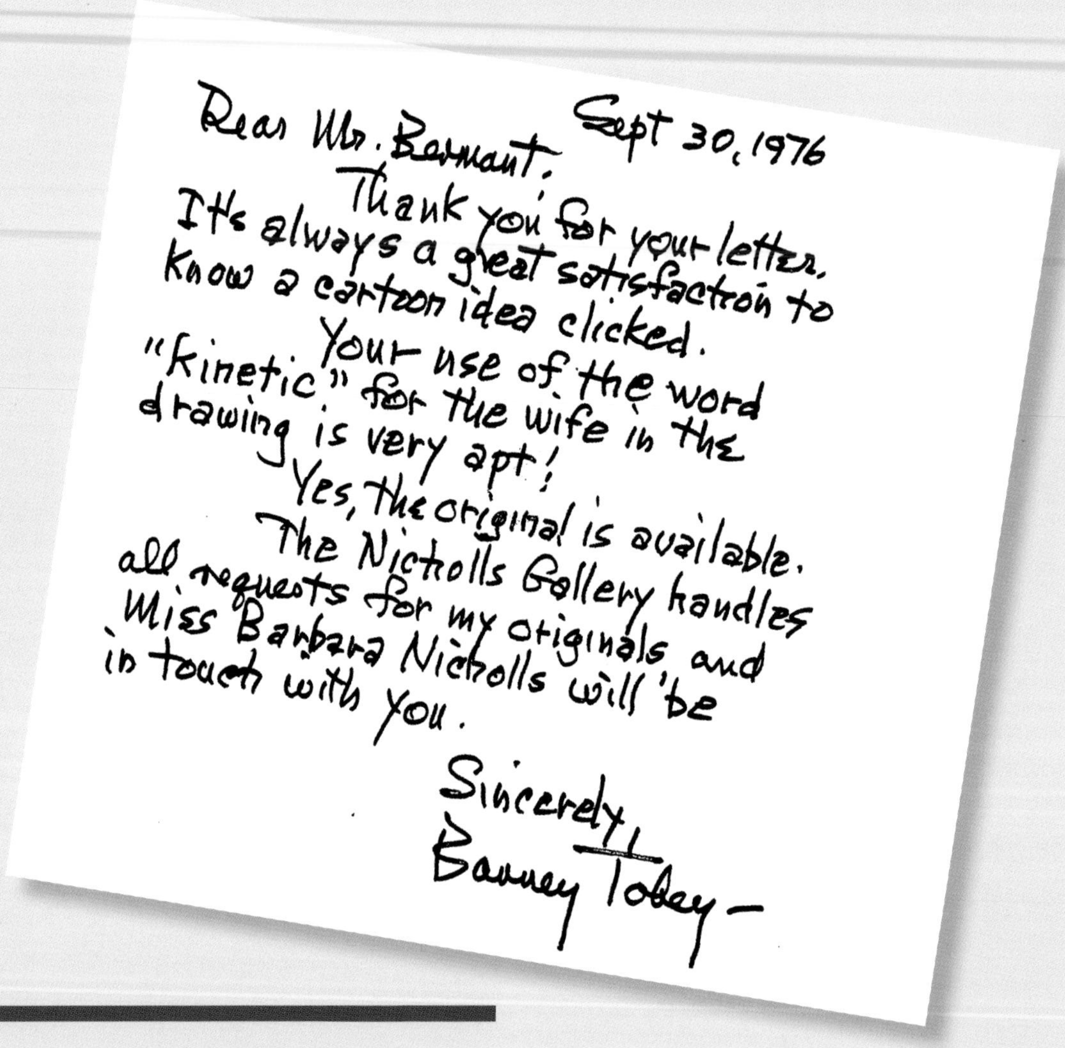

Sept 30, 1976

Dear Mr. Bermant,

Thank you for your letter. It's always a great satisfaction to know a cartoon idea clicked.

Your use of the word "kinetic" for the wife in the drawing is very apt!

Yes, the original is available. The Nicholls Gallery handles all requests for my originals and Miss Barbara Nicholls will be in touch with you.

Sincerely,
Barney Tobey —

"I look at Picasso or Henry Moore or Stella and I wonder why they're paying that kind of money for them. I'm not exactly welcome in the art circles, as you can well imagine."

—DWB

This note refers to cartoon on previous page spread.

"WELL, DAVID, THERE ARE A LOT OF THINGS TO LIKE ABOUT IT,"

" 'What the hell is wrong with me?' I wondered. 'Why am I the only one in the world who collects this form of art so intensely?' "
—DWB

THE COLLECTION

TECHNICAL CURATOR

CHRISTOPHER HOPMANS

Christopher Hopmans has been Technical Curator of the Bermant art collection since 1992. In addition to making sure all the pieces are in working order, he oversaw installation of the 1993 exhibition of the collection by the Butler Institute of American Art. One of his biggest challenges was packing and coordinating the move of the collection from Rye, New York, to its current location in California. Along with his resourcefulness and remarkable diversity of skills, Christopher has a wonderful sense of humor about the collection and a great affection for many of the pieces.

"When we moved the collection we didn't think it could be transported from New York to California without being destroyed. However, Christopher Hopmans, our Technical Curator, figured out a way to get it here splendidly."
—DWB

"I used to think nepotism was a bad thing, but now I don't!"

—Christopher Hopmans

"David loved his art and loved the fact that I could keep it working, so it made for a great relationship."

—Christopher Hopmans

"I insisted on being able to afford a technical curator before I ever began to collect this art. I think it was a wise move. Because if it doesn't work, you don't have art. I don't know what you got, but it ain't art."

—DWB

"For those who are not intimately familiar with the many 'technicalities' of technological art, I want to emphasize the very great demands upon the owner of a collection of this kind . . . Not only are many of the works extremely fragile, but the problems of installation and maintenance pose concerns and demands much greater than conventional works of art."

—Tracy Atkinson

"Most of the pieces in my collection work very well, but I do need a Technical Curator to make sure this is working and that is working. They do break down— they're mechanical. But what the hell? They're a part of our society. They come out of the technological discoveries of our society."

DWB

THE COLLECTION

"Your enthusiasm is infectious and is communicated beautifully by the spritely quality of the works you have acquired, their sense of humor, as well as thoughtful placement in the landscape."

—*Gallery visitor to DWB*

"The collection was a joy to see. Going into it I didn't really know what to expect. As the tour progressed it just got better and better, capturing my attention every moment."

—*Gallery visitor*

Thank You Collage
Judi Stauffer

"David was really in awe of how an artist came up with something. He always asked, 'How did you think of that? How did that come to you? How did you get that idea?' He was always fascinated with how you arrived at an idea. It's hard to explain how you do it, but it was something he had a deep appreciation for, that's for sure."

—James Wines

"David was interested in the survival of the artists he patronized. He was interested in their welfare, their life in general, whether they were gonna make it through the next year, whether they were eating three meals a day. He was that kind of person, in terms of personal generosity. He was also kind of a gruff person, probably a formidable foe in his real estate dealings. I'm sure he was a tough cookie when it came to dealing with that shopping center world. But with most of his artists he was incredibly generous and understood that we were really struggling to do something, usually for purely idealistic reasons."

—James Wines

"One last thing needs to be said. Your energetic and total commitment to us and our work, David, has not only renewed our commitment to it, but given us hope that it will be seen in our lifetimes as work that is some of the most important being done today. Your efforts must seem thankless at times, as ours do to us, but I have no doubt that the future will redeem it all."

—Letter from Clyde to DWB, October 26, 1981

EXHIBITIONS

WADSWORTH EXHIBITION CATALOG

Introductory Essay

David W. Bermant

Forty-five years ago, F.S.C. Northrop, Sterling Professor (Emeritus) of Philosophy and Jurisprudence of Yale University, convinced me, as well as others, that the most vital art of one's time was that art which incorporates the underlying reality of the world as discovered by the science of one's time.

This reality, as revealed by science and verified by experiment, has primary concepts or principles. Philosophy formulates these primary principles into a metaphysical system. This system's intellectual concepts, understandable but to a few, is converted by religion and art into concrete symbols which convey emotion and feeling to everyone.

For example, Aristotle's discovery of the foundation of biological organization was incorporated centuries later by St. Thomas of Aquinas into a metaphysical system that became the basic principles of Catholicism. These principles were clothed by Catholic religion and the art inspired by it into emotion-filled symbols and metaphors.

The primary concept, or underlying reality, of the science of our day is Relativity. Einstein added the fourth dimension to those of Newtonian physics: time. Therefore, the art of our day that incorporates time, or movement, motion, change, is the most vital of all the arts being created. It is the art of our time that will endure.

In addition, this art of movement uses the technology of its day as a tool in creating its aesthetic effect. It uses technology's materials, theories, and by-products; it celebrates it, criticizes it, even pokes fun at it. And how appropriate, since technology is surely the one feature unique to our society that distinguishes it from every other society heretofore.

Two thousand three hundred years ago, Aristotle urged his countrymen to place art in the ordinary, daily environment of their communities. Thus in the "agoras" or market places of ancient Greece, art was located along with commercial products.

Twenty years ago, based on the above principles, I began placing the art of movement and technology into the shopping centers that I own in partnership with others. They are located east of the Mississippi, and range in size from community size centers of an open "strip" nature to large regional enclosed malls. My objective was to make my centers more pleasant places to visit. Since most shopping centers look alike to me, I also feel that by adding an aesthetic dimension to an ordinary space, I am giving a special identity to my centers. I believe that, as a result, my centers will endure longer as viable economic entities. But why? What is it about art—and in particular this form of art—that endows an everyday public space with longevity?

Well, something strange has happened "on the way to the market place": the American public actually enjoys this form of art. It amuses; it amazes; in Ivan Karp's words "it engages the interest of the average person," thus widening the audience for the visual arts. The non-traditional materials it uses widen the scope of the subject matter of the visual arts—incorporating the very "stuff" of everyday living.

However, most of the art placed in public places in America up until now has been architecturally oriented (i.e., abstract art that relates to the architecture). If not actually chosen by the architect, its choice certainly has been influenced by him. In the case of the General Services Administration, he is the initiating element and is a member of every panel. Certainly there is nothing wrong with architectural art, per se, except for certain factors—too often it's what Calvin Tomkins has termed "plop art" ("the artist has simply taken one of his existing ideas or designs, blown it up in scale, and plopped it down in the lobby or plaza assigned to him.") It is infrequent that anyone responds to it outside of the architect, the owner, and the artist. I question its almost exclusive use in public buildings and plazas.

I propose that the art to be placed in public places be expanded to contain other forms of art—including, hardly incidentally, the art of movement that stems from the science and technology of our day.

It is my hope that this museum exhibition will bestow the necessary credentials upon the art I love in order that, in the words of Tracy Atkinson, I can help bring to the public places of America "a public art that is at once appealing to the general public and is truly distinguished in the art world."

"I believe one can find truth for one's time. One can find right and wrong for one's time. Maybe none of these are eternal, but they are to be found. I am going to try to seek out the truth as long as I live, and always tell the truth as long as I live, not only to others, but mostly to myself. I will never lie."
—DWB

WADSWORTH ATHENEUM

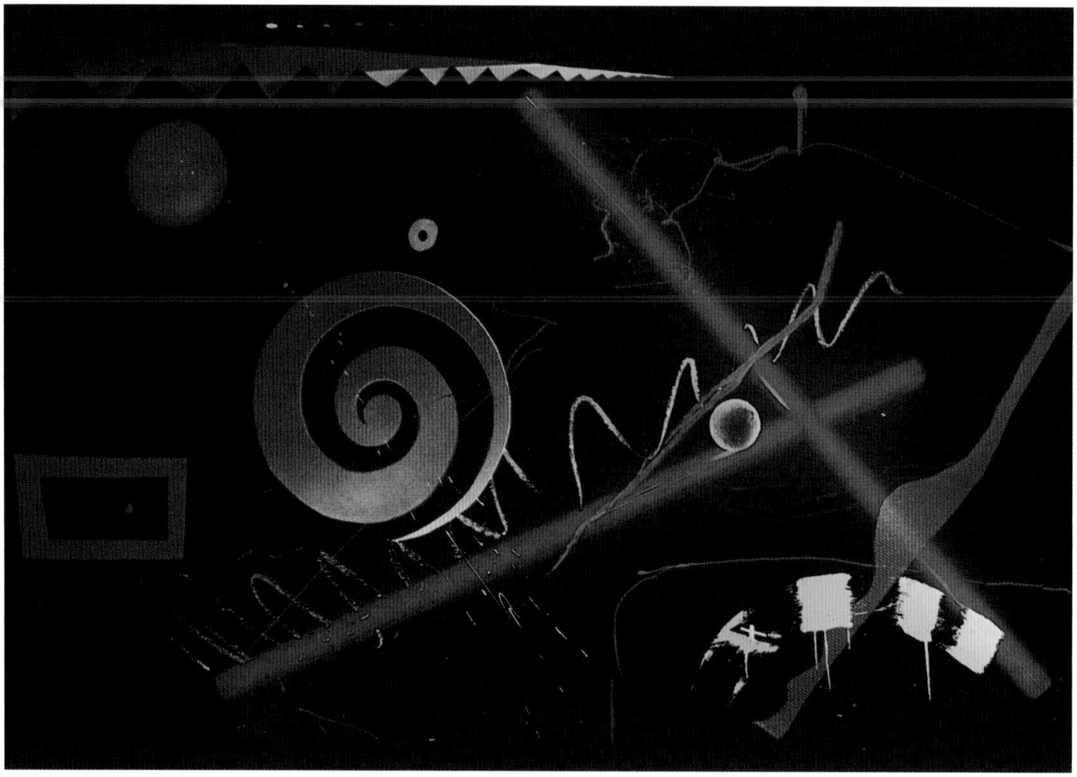

ART SPELLINGS
New Frontier
1984
48"H x 72"W x 10"D

DAVID BERMANT COLLECTION: COLOR LIGHT MOTION

Exhibition at Wadsworth Atheneum
1984

Installation and maintenance of this exhibition was made possible by the participation and cooperation of numerous artists, including Nam June Paik, James Seawright, Clyde Lynds, James Ossi, George Rhoads, Alejandro & Moira Siña, Ted Victoria, Tsai, Jenny Holzer, James Wines, Kristin Jones and Andrew Ginzel.

Located in the heart of downtown Hartford, Connecticut, the Wadsworth Atheneum is the oldest public art museum in the United States.

JENNY HOLZER
Truisms
1983
7"H x 60"W x 4"D

HAROLD LEHR
Water Sculptures
1972

COLOR, LIGHT, MOTION EXHIBITION

Catalog Introduction
By Tracy Atkinson, Director

This exhibition, like all exhibitions of private collections, is as much about the collector as it is about the art which is collected. David Bermant collects technological art and he also owns shopping centers. He is not alone in the world by virtue of either fact, but the way in which he combines these aspects of his life certainly makes him unusual if not unique.

Bermant believes that the most significant art for today expresses the scientific principles which represent the vanguard of human thought and which underlie the values of our time. He gives life to this belief by placing this kind of art in public places for all to experience. Further, he devotes considerable energy to getting others to follow suit by enabling artists to have the means to explore what is still, perhaps surprisingly, relatively uncharted waters.

Modern science and modern art have been exchanging values since the beginning of the century so the wonder is, I suppose, that there is not more technological art in the world.

"Analemma was our
very first permanent
commission, THANKS
TO DAVID!"

—*Kristin Jones*

JONES/GINZEL
Analemma
1988
Wadsworth Atheneum
10'H x 12'W x 6'D (overall)
Air, glass, lead, mineral oil,
sand, steel, aluminum, brass,
motors, timers, pigment,
copper, ammonium chloride,
incandescent light, gold

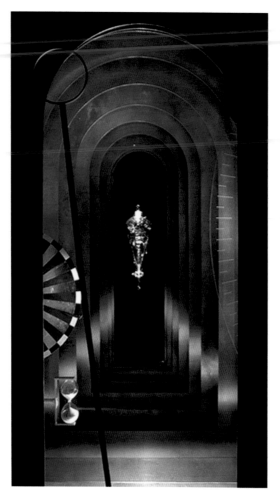

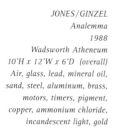

KRISTIN JONES AND ANDREW GINZEL

Jones holds a BFA in Sculpture from the Rhode Island School of Design and an MFA from Yale University. Ginzel teaches at the School of Visual Arts and lives and works in New York City. Individually and in collaboration, Kristin Jones and Andrew Ginzel have constructed installations and created site-specific works for museums, galleries, and architectural spaces throughout the world.

KRISTIN JONES ABOUT DWB:

I became acquainted with the whole collection of individuals who made up "his circle of artists." It was David who introduced us to one another. David was the center. He explained to me that he was not only an art collector, but he collected people too. I was fascinated by his sheer energy, absolute honesty, gut reactions, fearlessness, brazen gusto, and passionate sense of adventure. David had definite opinions; he immensely enjoyed lambasting curators and critics and had a definite rhetoric about "his art" about "his artists." There was no guessing what he might like; he either liked something or he did not. He was instinctual. It was refreshing for me to experience such flagrant honesty and conviction. I enjoyed witnessing how much fun David had, and I learned a great deal from going around with him to see art, watching him react.

David was very direct. Amidst our excursions to galleries and conversations with artists, he spoke of his pleasure in wine, food, and sex openly and discussed the many creatures of his desires!

David was so, so vibrant, so excited about life, and so open to discovery.

David changed my life absolutely! His commitment to PUBLIC, to ART and to ARTISTS was so rigorous. David was a huge inspiration to me both by example and through our enormous differences. There was always a conquest, something new he was trying or exploring: wine, art, even various diets and cures, bracelets, a new psychic . . . There was always a project in the air, a desire to be fulfilled to a greater and greater extent.

His sheer JOY and vitality was contagious. He loved telling stories.

From the time I first met David in the fall of 1985 until the fall of 1994 (when Andrew and I won the Rome Prize from the American Academy and went to Rome for a year) was a very productive time—VERY. It's that magic time in one's life when potential is so ripe—when you are exploding with energy. David's constant encouragement and sheer excitement was very much part of that time.

David purchased the first saleable work that Andrew and I created out of a group exhibition at the annual Invitational Exhibition at Grace Borgenicht Gallery in New York. The work, Apastron, is a celestial-terrestrial work. It is a 'wonder cabinet' with two large spheres turning in opposite directions, a stratigraphy of ash and coal on a Prussian blue field, and a very slow tick and tock wand that measures time. Analemma was our very first permanent commission, THANKS TO DAVID!

P.U.L.S.E. – NEW YORK

EXCERPT FROM "TODAY'S MACHINES"

P.U.L.S.E. Catalog
By Tom Finkelpearl, Curator

P.U.L.S.E.

ALICE AYCOCK
STEVE BARRY
MARCEL DUCHAMP
LEE JAFFE
KRISTIN JONES / ANDREW GINZEL
CLYDE LYNDS
GEORGE RHOADS
JAMES SEAWRIGHT
ALEJANDRO and MOIRA SINA
TAKIS
JEAN TINGUELY
TED VICTORIA
Curator: Tom Finkelpearl

APRIL 4 — MAY 23, 1987
420 WEST BROADWAY, NEW YORK, NY

a project of the
DAVID BERMANT FOUNDATION: COLOR, LIGHT, MOTION
coordinated through the
INSTITUTE FOR ART AND URBAN RESOURCES
and the
LOWER MANHATTAN CULTURAL COUNCIL

People Using Light, Sound, Energy

The parameters of this exhibition as stated in the title, "People Using Light, Sound, Energy," needs a bit of clarification. While all of the artists fall within the stated categories, there is no work that is solely sound or light. These two categories are now important subsets of visual arts and music, and there have been major exhibitions in both fields in recent years.

P.U.L.S.E. is essentially a sculpture show, artists who create sculptural objects from light, sound, and energy. Light art often tends toward painting, while sound art verges on music. In fact, a more accurate title might be Sculptures Using Light Sound Energy. The only thing constant in P.U.L.S.E. is change.

The artists in P.U.L.S.E. do not share a common attitude toward machines and computers. In some work we see the power and brutality of the machine, in others we see the beauty. However, all of the artists have turned to technology (whether low-tech or high-tech) to express themselves. The work seems to divide into three categories: artists who see the power and danger of the machine, those who stress the beauty of technology and those who do not address these issues, but simply explore potential uses of newly acquired techniques. For these artists, technology is a means to an end, not the subject of their work.

Steve Barry, Alice Aycock, Jean Tinguely, and Takis create machines that are at once violent and beautiful. This sort of work appeals to those who admire and/

"I have chosen to concentrate a selection of works, so that they represent one facet of the many trends now evident in today's art. The facet I have chosen is that of "technological art," which in simple terms, is the use of today's scientific discoveries—be they materials, relations, or principles—to produce objects of art."

or fear factory design, who see the terror and beauty in the sets of "Modern Times." There is nothing high-tech or computer driven in their work. In some sense, we can look at their production as a throwback to the machine age. a time when the adversary was steel gears not "user friendly" computer programs. Just as Charlie Chaplin's "Modern Times" are no longer modern, these artists are not creating work about the future. It is not surprising, then, that Barry draws his themes from classical texts, or that Aycock draws upon ancient cosmologies. Their work confronts modern issues, but not directly. The issues are stated in terms of man's eternal struggle with power, death and place within the cosmos. Takis and Tinguely, from an older generation, have a different outlook. While their work acknowledges the violence and beauty of machines, it is more abstract, less tied to a narrative. Lee Jaffe's work is an evocation of the terror of machines, but also the terror of nature (a more traditional theme in art).

George Rhoads and James Seawright celebrate the beauty of the machine and the computer. Rhoads creates playful non-functional machines. We are not threatened by the machines' movements or sound, only delighted. Seawright demonstrates the power of the computer. His works are computer driven, and he stresses the computer look. Like the Futurists, these artists embrace technology. Rhoads embraces the mechanical past, Seawright the micro-chip future.

The technology is a means to an end. In fact, in all of their work the mechanical aspects are hidden, irrelevant as aspects of the work except in that they

(continued on page 78)

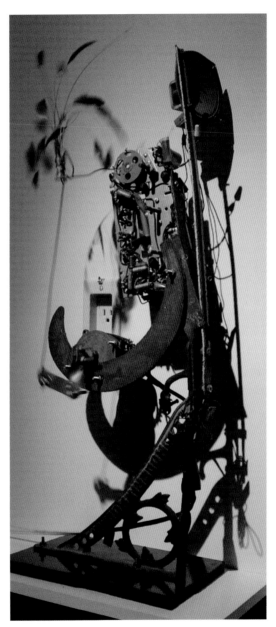

JEAN TINGUELY
Tokyo Gal
1967
29"H x 11"W x 6"D

"I have a Jean Tinguely piece I loaned to the Neuberger Museum. When I got there it was in a container. I said to the director, 'What the hell did you do this for? This piece is a fun piece. You're supposed to push a button and let it move and make the sounds it makes, otherwise you don't have a piece of art.' And she said, 'Well, I didn't want anyone to break it.' I said, 'Let them break it, we can fix it. This is a part of our society. We have to maintain our machines whether they're computers or art pieces.'"
—DWB

(continued)

create movement, light, or steam. In some ways, these artists represent a totally new approach. Without drawing attention to their use of technology, they create effects that would be impossible without it. Because mechanical sculpture is now sixty-seven years old, it is possible to create work in the medium without drawing attention to the medium.

"I must congratulate you on writing the clearest dissertation on the exhibit that I have seen yet. It is what I think criticism is supposed to be; not the gobbledygook that no one except the writer and a few chosen cohorts can understand."
—DWB (Letter to Julie Wosk, December 2, 1988)

JONES/GINZEL
Seraphim
1985

JONES/GINZEL
Thelion
1987

"That was a very important show because it happened at a time when there was a certain hiatus in what was going on in the art scene. It was right on West Broadway and happened to hit a moment when there wasn't much else going on, and it got a lot of attention and was even rated, I think, the best show of its kind for the season. I forget exactly what its bragging rights were, but it really was the first time that the art world in general got a focused look at what David was doing. They rented the ground floor of the building at 420 West Broadway, which was the building where Castelli had his gallery on the fourth floor. It was the prime location in SoHo, and SoHo was riding high at that time."

—*James Seawright about P.U.L.S.E. – New York*

NAM JUNE PAIK
Fish Tales
1986
42"H x 23"W x 21"D

ALDRICH MUSEUM

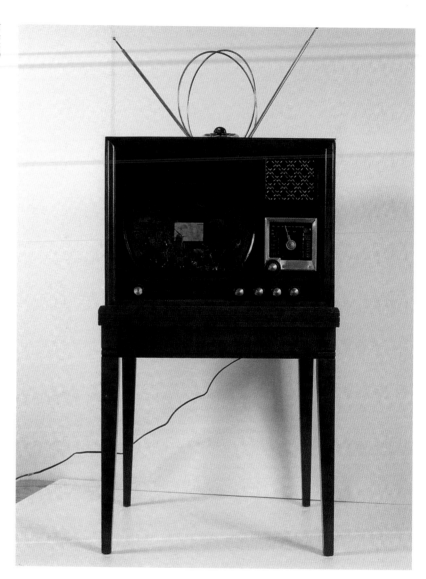

INTERACTION:
Light — Sound — Motion
1988 Exhibition

The Aldrich Contemporary Art Museum, located in Ridgefield, Connecticut, was founded by Larry Aldrich of New York City and Ridgefield. Exhibitions began in 1964, and the museum became known as a champion of new talent. It is a leader in presenting the world's best contemporary art and has a reputation for exhibiting highly innovative works by outstanding artists. In 1988 David Bermant supported the INTERACTION: Light — Sound — Motion exhibition and loaned several of his artworks for it. The exhibition included major works by twenty contemporary artists.

TED VICTORIA
God Bless America
1984–1988
Room installation consisting of
25 projectors and rear projection
screens.

INTERACTIVE ART

Miranda McClintic

This exhibition presents a broad spectrum of work. Some are meditative, several are humorous, and many have a magical quality. All of the work is sculptural but much of it has a strong pictorial component as well. Sound or light—and often both—are the common denominators of all the works and nothing in this show is static, not even light.

—Miranda McClintic
Excerpt from "Interactive Art"
Interaction Catalog

EXHIBITIONS

P.U.L.S.E. 2 – SANTA BARBARA

P.U.L.S.E. 2 — SANTA BARBARA

1990 Exhibition
Excerpt from catalog by Phyllis Plous, Curator

P.U.L.S.E. 2 marks a milestone both for the University Art Museum and the field of contemporary art as a whole. It constitutes a large-scale exhibition of light, sound, and energy sculpture that combines traditional gallery installations with site-responsive public art projects. A celebratory event, it is also the first collaboration between several major art institutions in the Santa Barbara area.

Too often since the late 1960s, interactive sculpture has been lumped together under the rubric of "kinetic art" and dismissed as amusing, déjà vu gadgetry.

Early in its organizational phase, David Bermant, a highly motivated, passionate collector of interactive sculpture, became an active supporter of the Museum's endeavor.

Second only to the artists in making this project possible is the diverse group of lenders. Particular gratitude goes to Mr. Bermant, founder, and James Seawright, president, of the David Bermant Foundation: Color, Light, Motion for their encouragement of this undertaking.

This project has been an expensive and difficult undertaking. In funding P.U.L.S.E. 2, the David Bermant Foundation: Color, Light, Motion and the University Museum Council have demonstrated their belief in sculpture that uses developing technologies as a significant area of contemporary art, both within conventional gallery spaces as well as in the public domain. We are grateful to them.

BASCHET BROTHERS
Musical Fountain
1974
58"H x 38"W x 38"D

"The things I appreciated most about David were his good taste, his optimism, his energy when he made a decision, and his humanity. I think his greatest strength was his energy, his tenacity when his decision was made."

—Francois Baschet
(March 5, 2009)

P.U.L.S.E. 2 – SANTA BARBARA REVIEW

Artweek (September 1990)
By Josef Woodard

P.U.L.S.E. 2 has taken over Santa Barbara, filling spaces at University of California, Santa Barbara, and downtown with art by People Using Light, Sound and Energy. Right down to the title's clever acronym, the show is a marketable proposition: art that moves or interacts almost automatically ensures populist appeal. The numbers speak volumes: the show lasts four months; eighty-six works by more than fifty artists are on display (including several large-scale sculptures), dispersed in six galleries around town, as well as scattered public locations. The most extensive exhibition ever undertaken in Santa Barbara P.U.L.S.E. 2— whatever its final effect—fulfills the purpose of a broad-based exhibition filtering out into the community.

DWB

"This art will either stand on its own and be recognized for being the quality that it is and being a part of our civilization, as it should be, or it will die. I'm going to try to make it live." (Interview with Mary Anne Christy, "Art & Auction")

JONES/GINZEL
Atoll – Pacific Lagoon Project
1990

VANDALISM OF CLYDE LYNDS' STELE LXXV, GNOMON

Santa Barbara News Press
Donald Murphy

The artwork was placed in front of the Lobero Theater as part of the P.U.L.S.E. 2 exhibition in Santa Barbara, mid-April. In late August it was toppled by a vandal and damaged beyond repair. Nancy Moore, Executive Director of the Lobero, said, "This was a wonderful piece and very popular. It was like a simple obelisk during the day, but at night it came alive."

"Probably nothing could be more impervious to weathering, destruction, etc. than my cement pieces; however, there is absolutely no way anyone could guarantee anything to withstand people."
—Clyde Lynds

ERIC ORR
Prime Matter VIII
1987
114"H x 9"W x 8"D

CLYDE LYNDS
Stele LXXV, Gnomon
1990

"I want to jerk this town out of the 18th and into the 20th century. Santa Barbara is a jewel of American cities. I want this art to add some glitter to the jewel."

DWB

EXHIBITIONS

BUTLER INSTITUTE

LOU ZONA, EXECUTIVE DIRECTOR, BUTLER INSTITUTE OF AMERICAN ART

"David offered to show his collection at the Butler and that was the beginning of a full-fledged dedication to the Butler toward art and technology, culminating in the creation of the Bermant Gallery which has been a showcase for art based upon technology since 2000."

Lou to DWB: "The James Seawright mirrored piece, which you so kindly gave to the Butler, continues to be the favorite permanent collection piece with children. All day long we hear children reacting to it. It's been a great addition."

Lou to DWB: "Every piece that you have given us is on display—we love them! People still come in and ask where the Bermant collection exhibition is. It obviously made a tremendous impact when it was here five years ago."

"David continues to be our inspiration and I tell you, every time we install a new show in the Bermant Gallery I think about David and what he might've thought about this particular exhibition. He's very much alive at the Butler Institute and the Bermant Gallery continues to be the most exciting spot in the museum."

THE BUTLER INSTITUTE OF AMERICAN ART
FOUNDED   1919

Louis A. Zona
Director

524 Wick Avenue, Youngstown, Ohio 44502
Telephone (216) 743-1107 FAX: (216) 743-9567

November 26, 1993

David Bermant
Via Fax

Dear David,

On behalf of the Board of Trustees of the Butler Institute, I offer you our sincere thanks for your most generous loan of selections from your technological art collection. The show, in its year-long run at the Butler Institute, was seen by over one hundred-twenty thousand museum visitors of all ages. From the youngest viewer to retirees, the show was praised as the best exhibition hosted by the Butler to date, and the musuem staff and I agree with that assessment.

Additionally, the response of the press and local media was very positive, with the consensus being that the show proved that visual artists are indeed in touch with the phenomenal growth of scientific knowledge of our century. Your collection is truly "in touch" with our age and what people really wish to experience in our country's museums.

On a personal level, I never tired of the exhibition and was probably its most faithful fan. When my staff wanted to find me during the past year and couldn't, it was because I was in the north galleries viewing the Clyde Lynds or Milton Komisar.

Thank you again. I hope that we will be able to work together again soon on another project. My best to you for the new year.

Sincerely,

Lou Zona

LZ/ke

"He was so devoted to the artists he collected. He was so proud of each and every one of them and bragged about them as if they were his children. I never forgot that, that level of support, and I think they really appreciated it, and I think they knew that they had a true friend and supporter in David Bermant."
—Lou Zona

I AM A BRIDGE

By David W. Bermant

I am a Bridge, a connection between the art form that has been described to you on the panel this morning, and the public spaces of America, in particular my shopping centers.

About twenty years ago, I began placing this form of art in my centers. The art that I promoted or advocated the use of in public spaces is different because it's not art that just has a technological connection. It's art that comes out of the technology and/or science of our time. It can consist of the materials or the stuff of everyday living—the products of a technological society.

It's been my observation, and that of others, that the art works that have been placed in public areas up until now have been largely rejected by the very public that they were intended to attract.

There are special public moods to the art because of the audience that the art appeals to. It needs explanation. In a shopping center or in a public square, or in a corporate building, labels are vital. Labeling helps the non-art lover, who is 99 percent of the public, to understand what the art is about, what it's trying to do—and it helps them enjoy it. Second, it helps protect the art by labeling it as, "It's art."

There are some compromises that are necessary in order to be able to place art in public spaces. The construction by the artist must take into consideration the needs of the space. The area where the art is located must be kept conspicuously clean. But what protects these art objects is the sense of community pride. This develops from the fact that the community has within its midst, in one of its very ordinary everyday spaces, an aesthetic collection that lifts it above ordinary places, makes it an aesthetic dimension that is appreciated by the community, and they become proud of it. They talk about it to their friends, their neighbors, and their visitors. When they see it reinforced by special articles that appear in their local papers and in national magazines and over national TV, this pride is further reinforced.

Public art spaces require variation—how often can you see the same darn piece? Yet, neither publicly owned spaces nor privately owned spaces such as shopping centers can afford constantly changing art displays, such as a museum or an art gallery does. I believe that our form is superior to most other art forms because the variations occur within the pieces themselves—the content differs, the aesthetic experience differs, and it's more beautiful or less beautiful within each single piece.

Therefore, I hope that you will join with me wherever you can in helping me advocate the use of this art in the public spaces of America for one, principle objective, that is as Aristotle said, "The end of the goal is the same as the defined goal of fine art. The goal of the end of fine art is that certain pleasurable impression produced upon the mind or the eyes of the viewer." And I hope that when you come to the public spaces that I'm placing this art in, you too will feel a sense of pleasure by feeling good about being here.

DWB

"I served five years in the United States Army. The last year I was in active combat, and I saw guys die right next to me. Somehow, the good Lord preserved me, and I said to myself, 'If I ever make enough money that I can be free to do what I want to do, I'm going to try to make the country I live in, that I love so much, and that these poor guys died for, a better place to be.' I know that sounds corny, and I don't care if it sounds corny. That's the way I feel."
—DWB, 1984 TV interview

SHOPPING CENTERS

ALLENDALE

Gentlemen:

In regards to Dustin Shuler's "Sea Bee", the controversial assemblage at the Allendale Center, I have only one comment:

I love it!
I love it!
I love it!
I love it!
I love it!
I love it!
I love it!
I love it!
I love it!
I love it!
I love it!
I love it!
I love it!
I love it!
I love it!
I love it!
I love it!
I love it!

Sincerely,

Winni Neveu

Allendale Shopping Center is located in Pittsfield, Massachusetts. Originally opened in 1955 it was purchased in 1973 by National Shopping Centers and managed by Joseph Bermant.

November 23, 1990

Ms. Winifred Neveu
The House at Harbor Bend
170 East View Drive
RFD Adams, Mass. 01220

Dear Ms. Nevue:

Thank you!
Thank you!
Thank you!
Thank you!
Thank you!
Thank you!
Thank you!
Thank you!
Thank you!
Thank you!
Thank you!
Thank you!
Thank you!
Thank you!
Thank you!
Thank you!
Thank you!
Thank you!

Sincerely,

David W. Bermant

DWB/sp

"Bermant says, 'I want to bring fine art into the public spaces of America.' But he admits there's a commercial advantage to having such lures. The artwork is carefully placed to encourage shoppers to walk or elevate down into the Allendale Underground—the newest section of the shopping center."

—(Newspaper article)

THE SEA BEE

By Justin DiPego

"The Sea Bee" stood high on its end, the prow arcing toward the sky. Towering over the asphalt sea, it could be seen to be sinking by the bow, or emerging triumphantly from the depths. Of all his works, this was Dustin Shuler's favorite.

Shuler spent three months in Boston Harbor. He acquired an actual fueler tender, a ship built to maintain and fuel fishing vessels. Since 1948, "The Sea Bee" had plied its trade on Massachusetts waters. By 1990, it was a derelict hulk, resting on the sand, sinking twice a day in high tide.

Working with his crew, Shuler cut off and rebuilt thirty-two feet of the bow. Bright red paint went on below the water line. Shining black was the hull. The deck was washed with eye squinting white. Hauled to Pittsfield, Massachusetts, the 15-ton structure was erected in the parking lot of Bermant's Allendale Shopping Center.

The public was divided. While many saw the romance of Shuler's vision, others were troubled by the idea of a sinking icon in the economically sinking town. Ultimately, the center was sold, and in 2002, "The Sea Bee" was taken down. Shuler cut off the forward eight feet and erected it in the grass outside the library at California State University, Fullerton.

DUSTIN SHULER
The Sea Bee
1990

"If you can start a person's day, or end their day, with a smile . . . I think that's a pretty good function for a fine art object."

GEORGE RHOADS

"Having a Ball" was located next to the glass elevator in Allendale Shopping Center, allowing passengers to view the art while they rode up and down in the elevator. Balls moved windmills as they traveled back to the ball lift; metal and wood organ pipes added sound. This audio-kinetic sculpture was a delightful piece of art for visitors of all ages.

DWB

"George's works are easily the most popular artwork in each public area, whether shopping center, airport, or bus terminal. Since they are accessible (an art term meaning 'easily understood') to anyone of any age, group, race, or economic class, they are the first art objects I introduce into my shopping centers. They bring smiles to anyone capable of smiling. Is bringing a smile to one's face in this complicated and anxiety-ridden world an unworthy objective of a fine art piece?"

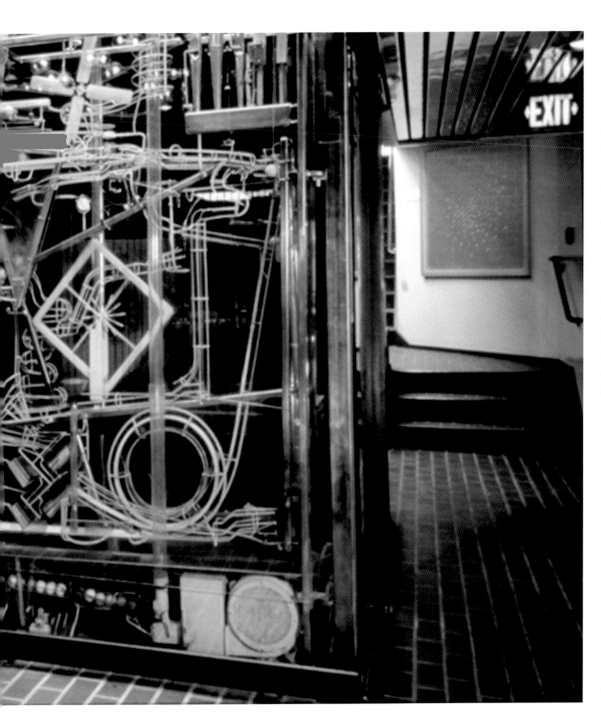

"Nothing is represented, but you could think of different interpretations. The main one . . . the balls are the soul going through incarnations. Start with birth at the top and death at the bottom. So each time the ball goes through, it goes a different way; it does different things. It's a model of human existence—a model of collective existence, the picture of many souls in the Universe, or one soul in a succession of incarnations."

—George Rhoads

GEORGE RHOADS
Having a Ball
1983

DAVID DURLACH DESCRIBES "DANCING TREES"

"This sculpture is a controllable kinetic landscape which weaves metal and magnetism into music and dance. It is a 9-inch by 9-inch grid of cactus-like objects made of permanent magnets that self-organize into delicate spikes above a latticework of magnets. The iron powder covering the tray is quite light and has a very fast response time, allowing it to spring to life in a variety of performances as it 'dances' to the music."

DAVID DURLACH
Dancing Trees
1992
67"H x 77"W x 38"D

DAVID DURLACH TO DWB (1991)

"Your installation is by far the largest and most complex task I have ever taken on, primarily as a consequence of its having to be simultaneously vandal-resistant, weatherproof, portable, relatively quiet, field-repairable, and visually attractive as well. It has been required that I learn about topics as disparate as galvanic corrosion of dissimilar metals, marine grade acoustic damping foam, international copyright law, thermoelectric air conditioners, stainless steel grating material (to prevent rodents from making their nests and pissing in the warm a/c vent area), stainless steel leveling feet and many many other topics too numerous to mention."

"I must tell you that 'Dancing Trees' was a great success; people still come by and ask about it, little children weep and moan and adults gnash their teeth because it is no longer here . . . I just want you to know that it is probably the most successful art work that we have had here for quite awhile. I know that you are quite proud of this work, and you should know that the people of this area are very enthused."

—Joseph Bermant (DWB's brother) to David Durlach

"I want to thank you for all your intense efforts which I think resulted in one of the master works of our time. We shall show it with great pride."
—DWB (Letter to David Durlach, 1992)

SHOPPING CENTERS

NANCY RUBINS
Big Bil-Bored
1990

CERMAK PLAZA

THE ART & HISTORY OF CERMAK PLAZA

By David Aldrich

What in the world would ever cause a strip mall to become famous? You can spruce them up, modernize them, give 'em facelifts, and there's not the remotest chance these things will bring fame. No, it takes something drastic. And that's exactly what happened in the case of Cermak Plaza, a circa-1956 shopping center in Chicago's suburbs, when it became home to some huge (and hugely controversial) modern art pieces in the 1980s.

My first exposure to Cermak Plaza came around 1975, when my family moved from the Northwest suburbs to the Near West suburbs. One day, I noticed some scaffolding in the Cermak Plaza parking lot, surrounding what looked for all the world like a giant mud pie on a pedestal. As it turned out, what was taking place was the creation of a gigantic piece of modern art, the work of Nancy Rubins, an artist based in New York City's Soho district. The "pork chop shaped" sculpture, called "Big Bil-Bored," would stand three stories tall and was embedded with the flotsam of the American consumer culture—old portable televisions,

(continued on page 98)

SHOULD BIG BIL-BORED BE PRESERVED?

79% of the voters this spring voted against its remaining in Berwyn.

It cannot be removed without being DESTROYED.

A national polling company will conduct a survey to find out what YOU think.

The following dialogue may be helpful in reaching your conclusion.

BIG BIL-BORED – WHAT'S IT ALL ABOUT?

"Looks like a pile of junk to me."

"It is a pile of junk."

"Yeah? I thought they were telling us it was some kind of 'art'."

"Maybe it is some kind of art."

"Come on! It's junk and it's art? How can you figure that? Make up your mind, buddy."

"Well, how about this: It's made out of junk, which is not art just like the 'Old Masters' paintings were made out of canvas and paint which was not art … but what they did with it turned it into art."

"The artist starts out with some idea or message or story that they want to put across. They take whatever material they like to work with … paint and canvas, clay, a block of wood, a chunk of marble … or even a pile of worn out junk, and work it up to tell that story or put across that idea or message. The 'Old Masters' paintings usually had messages about the Bible or from mythology or about significant events or people. They were things that were important or of interest to the royalty, nobility or wealthy people of those times. The art work was for the people rich enough to pay for it, not the general public, and was seen in the churches or in the palaces and mansions of the rich."

"Uh huh. And what's that to do with this junk art?"

"In modern times artists have used a lot of different materials and new and surprising methods of putting across their ideas and messages. Sometimes they don't do a specific picture of it, but instead put together some clues and hints or suggestions and leave it up to us viewers to figure out the story."

"So what's the story this weirdo art's telling?"

"What do you think? What do you see here?"

"I see hundreds of pieces of junk; worn out and busted appliances, gadgets, machinery and household stuff all piled up."

"How does that make you feel?"

"Depressed. Irritated. Kind of mad."

"Why?"

"It's a mess! A big waste; costs a lot to make and buy all that stuff and here it is all of a sudden, useless junk all stacked up."

"So what do you suspect the artist's message might be?"

"Maybe that too many factories make too much stuff that doesn't last very long?"

"Could be. What else?"

"That we all get conned into buy a lot of stuff we don't need … or even really want … and it ends up in a junk pile too soon."

"Anything else?"

"… and we're running out of places to dump it all."

"And that's it?"

"How about we're using up all our natural resources and wasting it on junk? I hear about that a lot lately."

"So it turns out that you knew what the artist's message was all along and you just had to sort it out and think about it a little.."

"Yeash. Well, OK … but the whole bit still bugs me."

"Maybe it's supposed to bug you. Maybe it's meant to keep reminding you … and me … and everyone, that we're making too much stuff for our own good and some changes need to be made in what we think is important."

"Maybe so, maybe so. Let me think about it."

By Walt Hopmans, Art Historian and Educator

Santa Barbara, California

"The junk sculpture is of the highest art because it is honest, a revelation and a vision. It is rejected for those reasons by people who cannot bear to view themselves reflected in the sculpture's honesty, naked as consumers of American trash. Residents hate 'Bil-Bored' because they don't like hearing the truth about themselves—that they have devoted their lifetimes to the mass production of garbage. As a work of art, the sculpture is brilliant. It does not pretend to be beautiful, elaborate, or uplifting. It is what it is: a monument to what Americans create best—garbage. As a Berwyn resident, I love the junk sculpture."

—From Life newspaper, "Staff Views" column, June 21, 1981, by Randy Blaser

(continued)

fans, bicycles, hubcaps and other debris. The work was commissioned by Cermak Plaza owner David W. Bermant, an enthusiastic, high-profile patron of modern art. When the inevitable press questions came, Bermant responded from a socio-cultural perspective one doesn't generally expect from shopping center owners: "People can look at Nancy's work and see their own life," he told the *Chicago Tribune* in November 1980, as the sculpture neared completion. "At first I thought the plaza merchants would kill me. This piece shows the stuff they sell for what it is. But I decided to do it anyway because it was important."

As you would probably expect, the community went apoplectic over the sculpture. "It's a hunk of junk, a monstrosity," according to one angry resident quoted in the *Tribune* article. "Why don't those people do something constructive like sweeping the street instead of dirtying it up?" Judy Baar Topinka, the local state representative, weighed in on behalf of her constituents to the Berwyn/Cicero *Life* newspaper: "Is this the image that Berwyn wants to present to the world, a portal on a major thoroughfare? Instead of rejuvenation, revitalization, beautification, and progress, the message that is being sent is that we're riding high on the scrap heap. It is, at best, the worst public relations move I have ever seen put forth." Finally the mayor of Berwyn, Thomas Hett, conceded that due to the fact that it was on private property, little could be done. "But let me tell you, I don't see how anyone in their right mind could have approved the thing." In any event, "Big Bil-Bored" was there to stay.

My own attitude towards the sculpture was initially very negative, and I wish I could say that type of art

has grown on me in the years since, although in time I kind of got a kick out of all those 1950's-era toasters staring at me as I walked out of Walgreens or Service Merchandise. What has changed is that I've come to greatly admire Bermant's courage in daring to stand out from the crowd—a bold and exciting move, worthy of note.

Over the following decade, Bermant would commission several more modern art pieces, most much smaller, for Cermak Plaza. One that can still be seen at the Plaza is artist Dustin Shuler's "Pinto Pelt," which is essentially the hide of a Ford Pinto, mounted taxidermy-style to the side of the Plaza optometrist's shop. Given the Pinto's unfortunate reputation, that's probably the safest place for it.

The next large piece of modern art to appear at Cermak Plaza wasn't a sculpture or statue, but a building. In the spring of 1984, a new McDonald's restaurant with a unique design was built. Designed by SITE, which according to a *Tribune* article was "an art and architecture organization known for its exploration of new ideas for the urban visual environment," sections of the store were elevated, leading to an unusual "floating" appearance. Much credit for the modern design, of course, must go to Bermant, who "encouraged them to build a restaurant that would excite interest in the center and would complement the art works that we have already placed at Cermak."

The crowning achievement, as far as Cermak Plaza's art works went, would have to be "Spindle," built in 1989 by L.A.-based artist Dustin Shuler, who also created the "Pinto Pelt." "Spindle" consisted of eight cars impaled

(continued on page 100)

Floating McDonald's
SITE

MCDONALD'S WITH A DIFFERENCE BY SITE

Douglas Davis

Douglas Davis, architectural critic for *Newsweek*, in an article with the above heading in the December 24, 1984, issue, asked: "What happens when the hamburger giant puts itself in the hands of the most audacious architects alive?"

"Radical reversal is precisely what SITE has done to McDonald's standard design. While all the familiar parts are still there, they are dramatically altered. From afar, the new emporium seems poised for flight.

The roof floats weightlessly above the rest of the building. Parts of the façade are raised above the ground on unobtrusive steel piers; the resulting gaps are paneled with glass, exposing the feet and legs of customers inside to passers-by.

"Dubbed the 'Floating McDonald's,' the razzle-dazzle structure is attracting gapers and tourists. For the first time, McDonald's is a magnet for devotees of architecture as well as of hamburgers."

"We refused to allow McDonald's to put a store in our center unless they agreed to use one of our artist architects. Finally, after a great deal of negotiation they agreed to use the SITE organization."
—DWB

(continued)

on a giant metal spike, like a stack of skewered "guest checks" next to the cash register of a restaurant. Even though it no longer exists, "Spindle" is easily the most recognized image associated with Cermak Plaza.

Just as controversy surrounded the introduction of Cermak Plaza's most notable art works, "Big Bil-Bored" and "Spindle," it also surrounded their demise. "Big Bil-Bored," having survived nearly two decades of public outrage and various attempts to force its removal, was becoming an appreciable safety hazard due to severe rusting of its embedded metal artifacts. In 1998, it was dismantled. Guess they just don't make junk like they used to.

The destruction of "Spindle," which through the years had become a true Berwyn trademark, caused more consternation. In 2007, Walgreens made known its desire to build a free-standing store with a drive-thru pharmacy at the edge of the shopping center's parking lot. The spot they had in mind, as reported at the time, was exactly where "Spindle" stood. This time, there were allies in the battle—the Berwyn Arts Council and the Berwyn Mainstreet Committee headed up a valiant attempt to raise money to move the sculpture to another location within the parking lot in order to accommodate the new Walgreens store. On July 22, 2007, participants in Chicago Critical Mass, a monthly bike ride that attracts hundreds of cyclists, descended on Cermak Plaza to raise awareness of the need to "Save the Spindle," citing anger about "corporate interests erasing (the) town's identity." It would be to no avail. The decision was made to sell the sculpture on Ebay, but the auction, with a $50,000 starting bid, found no takers. On May 2, 2008, it came down.

"If you are not remembered for your charms and good looks, you will be remembered as a troublemaker and cultural hero."

—Ivan Karp, letter to DWB, January 15, 1981

"KEEP THE CAR SPIKE!"

"It is ugly urban art—but I like it. Keep the Spindle."

"I've been in the military since 1998, and people still ask me about the 'stacked cars' in 'Wayne's World' and if that was real or fake."

"The Spindle is one of the first things I ever saw that made me say, 'Whoa! That's so cool!' I never really appreciated the arts before."

"Other than being 40–50 feet tall it may not qualify as 'high art' but it celebrates, with a nice touch of humor, the importance of the automobile in our culture. It's a classic piece of folk art that we need to keep. Bravo, Spindle!"

"How many Walgreens do we have?? How many Spindles do we have??"

"We need to do all we can to keep the cars on the stick (as my kids call it)."

"Picasso it ain't but it does suit the character of the Plaza."

"The Spindle is one of the great pieces of modern art in this day and age. Tearing that marvelous piece of work down would be a terrible, terrible deed."

Two thousand bicyclists, part of Chicago Critical Mass, rode fifteen miles to the Spindle to protest replacing the Spindle with a Walgreens. Once at the Spindle they circled it repeatedly, chanting "Save the Spindle."

DUSTIN SHULER & DWB

By Justin DiPego

If it doesn't move, it's not art. That's how David W. Bermant put it. That may sound too definite to you, too limiting, but DWB was not an art scholar, he was an art lover. Surely on the face of it, much of the art he collected and commissioned moves, but a good deal of it only seems to move. The fact that these static pieces find their way into his personal gallery proves that he was right. One way or another, every piece in the collection moved him, from the very first he acquired, a brushed aluminum optical illusion, to the last, a scrap-metal sculpture collage of a cowboy roping a calf.

The perfect example of this is "Spindle," erected in 1989 by the artist, Dustin Shuler. In fact, run an internet search for David Bermant or Dustin Shuler and "Spindle" will be right at the top of the hit list. It didn't move, but it surely moved a lot of people. In the parking lot of a shopping center in Berwyn, Illinois, stood a fifty-foot spike, run through the bodies of eight cars. The cars stood aloft over this suburb of Chicago for nineteen years, made it into the movie "Wayne's World," became a tourist attraction, drew shoppers into the center and fostered love and hate from the community.

From the moment it went up, there were people demanding it be taken down. Most of them complained that it was not art. What they didn't realize was that by making that claim, they were proving themselves wrong. If you asked Shuler, he would put it this way, "Beauty is in the eye of the beholder and people think art is in the eye of the beholder—well, no it isn't. Art is based on the intent of the artist." If the intent is there, that makes it

(continued on page 102)

(continued)

art, not necessarily good art, but art nonetheless.

Trouble was brewing in Cermak Plaza. The shopping center was host to many works and the most infamous was a sculpture called, "Big Bil-Bored." Nancy Rubins' piece was a testament to consumerism. A 100-ton concrete structure, shaped like a pork chop and pocked with a mosaic of toasters, radios, blenders, desk fans and just about any and every other small appliance you can think of. It stood forty feet high in the lot and, as DWB simply put it, "My public hated it with a passion."

"It's a good thing you don't live here, Bermant," people would call him up to say. "You don't have to look at this thing every day."

"Don't look at it," DWB replied. "Look the other way and you don't have to be bothered by it."

"Big Bil-Bored" stood on private property so there was nothing the citizens or the city could do. "That course didn't exactly make me popular," said DWB, but he stuck to his guns. Controversy is not just in the nature of art, sometimes it is its purpose. Unlike "Spindle," "Big Bil-Bored" had little local support or sentimental attachment. People were not driving out of their way to take their picture in front of it.

After ten years of complaints and petitions from shoppers and aldermen a referendum was held. DWB agreed that if the majority of voters wanted the sculpture removed, he'd do just that. The answer came back 79 percent of voters in favor of removal. But DWB commissioned his own poll. The Gallup Organization conducted a study of a larger population at the same time as the public vote. They returned a different result. Fifty-one percent of people surveyed indicated the sculpture should be retained. Since his agreement with the city was that a clear majority must want the removal, and the two results didn't match up, DWB declared victory for the sculpture. "Big Bil-Bored" would stay.

In the midst of this, DWB looked into the huge parking lot at Cermak Plaza and knew it needed something more. He called Dustin Shuler, "Kid, I got a shopping center with a huge parking lot . . . I want something spectacular in there. What do you got?"

Shuler had been thinking of "Spindle" for years. He'd built a model. Now was the time. He had a photo. He handed it to DWB and said, "How's this?"

"Yeah," considered DWB. "Yeah, I think that would do it." And then he said, "How much?" Shuler had no idea. So, DWB offered, "Here's a thousand dollars. Find out."

How do you impale nine cars on a spike? How do you keep it from falling over? How do the cars stay in place? What kind of materials will it take? How much time? What will that cost? Shuler slogged his way through and came up with his figures. He submitted his findings, including his fee. DWB said, "Fine," and they took it from there.

Actually, that's the simple version; two no-nonsense men who get the job done and do it on a handshake. After that handshake came a contract and that can get rough, even, or especially, among friends. When DWB commissioned a piece, he kept the copyright. That's good business. Shuler gave up the copyrights on the two Pintos, but he didn't like it. Shuler always kept his copyrights. That's good business too.

Because of the expense of constructing "Spindle," Shuler wouldn't make much money on it. His fee was not the issue. He had no problem with that. But, "I knew what it was," Shuler said. "I knew this was gonna be a monument. This was gonna go around the world." With the copyright in hand, he could make up for the money that wouldn't come from the commission.

Shuler asked why DWB wanted to keep the copyright. It turned out, he was concerned that Shuler would do another "Spindle" somewhere else. Shuler said that was no problem and they put it in the contract: Shuler kept the copyright and in return promised not to produce another "Spindle." DWB in turn promised that the work would be safe for ten years. That way, if anyone tried to force DWB to remove it he could say, "Oh, no. I have a contract with the artist."

The theory here was based on DWB's belief that a work, particularly one with the potential for controversy, needed time to live in the community. People had to get used to it. It had to grow on them and (maybe) they'd come to love it. After ten years, if they hated it still, maybe it's time to take it down. Ultimately, "Spindle" survived for nineteen years.

Permits took a year. Shuler built more models. The city was fighting them; another giant sculpture in the same parking lot as "Big Bill Bored." They handed down a height restriction: fifty feet. The nine-car spire would stand fifty-four feet. Swallowing a special attachment to the number nine, Shuler knocked off one car.

Now eight cars had to be purchased, modified and skewered. These were real cars. A newspaper did a story before the construction and called it a "junkyard in the sky," but these were not junkers. To prove it, DWB offered up his own car to the project. As he put it, "the owner's car, donated to the art world."

Engines were taken out so they would balance properly. Drive trains and seats were removed to make way for the holes to be cut and the spindle to pass through. Gas tanks were removed so the sculpture wouldn't be a giant bomb.

From bottom to top, the cars were a black '79 Mercury Grand Marquis; a yellow '79 Ford LTD; a maroon '81 Pontiac Grand Prix; a two tone, white over blue, '78 Mustang II; a green '74 Mercury Capri; and a blue '81 Ford Escort. The next car was DWB's silver 1976 BMW New Class 1602. He wanted the car on top, but Shuler had his own idea. The BMW was the second car down and the whole thing was topped with a red 1967 VW Bug, like the cherry on a sundae.

As a thank you and a mollification, the artist made a special license plate for the BMW. It read, "DAVE."

Four pilings were sunk over a dozen feet into the earth. A foundation was laid. The spindle was erected, secured by a six foot dome of concrete at its base.

In part, the plaque at the foot of the spire read: "The automobile, the computer, and the television are the three technological wonders of the Twentieth Century that have most profoundly influenced our culture.

"Artist Dustin Shuler, with his finger on the pulse of the Twentieth Century, has chosen the automobile as the subject matter of his art.

(continued on page 104)

(continued)

"Spindle lifts the auto out of its ordinary place, and by relocating it as we've never seen before causes us to look again—to question its priority and importance in our daily living. Is it an object for veneration? If so, should it be?"

What better subject for art, Shuler put it, than the most dangerous thing you deal with on a daily basis? Public reaction was immediate and divided. "Spindle" became a landmark and a tourist attraction. People loved it. They were fascinated. Thousands attended a rally to preserve it when it was due to be knocked down and replaced by a Walgreens. Walgreens won out and "Spindle" is gone but it was in a shopping center after all. DWB challenged perceptions by inserting art into settings of working class commerce and he welcomed the controversy. In a voice that was both gruff and sprightly he said, "If you don't like it enough to go into my shopping center, stay the hell out. I don't care." But he was also a businessman and a good one. He knew that having art in his centers attracted 30 percent more business than a shopping center without it.

Despite that 30 percent bump in business, "There are much easier ways to make money." DWB had a vision and a mission to take art back to the streets. In his gruff and charming manner, he swiped Art from the cabinets and walls and pedestals of socially remote museums and smacked it into the path of the every-day American. In his shopping centers, the public was exposed to art without taking a special trip up the marble steps of a staid and sanctioned institution. No official voice told them what is good, what is worthy, what is art. Love it or hate it, it was theirs to experience, for them and of them.

Opposite:
GEORGE RHOADS
Bee Tree
1984
Cermak Plaza

BARRY MILLER
Moonbells
1985
Cermak Plaza

STEPHEN GERBERICH
Helicopter
Cermak Plaza

MOIRA SHEEHAN
Crosswalks
1990
Cermak Plaza

HAMDEN PLAZA

DUSTIN SHULER'S CAR PELTS

By Justin DiPego

Bermant was always trying to find a balance between the art world and the business world, and when he made that first visit to Shuler's shop, he had such a balancing act in mind. He owned Hamden Plaza, a shopping center in Connecticut, but he was contractually unable to change the sign. So, what could he do to the sign without changing it? He put the question to Shuler. What could he do?

At the time, the work Shuler was most known for was skinned cars. He pulled out all the innards, peeled the metal from the body and splayed it flat like a butterfly pinned to a corkboard.

So, that's what he could do for the sign. Leave the sign intact and drape a skinned green Pinto over the side like hanging a leopard pelt over the back of a chair.

Before that one was even finished, Bermant ordered another. Shuler looked out his office window and saw a car parked outside. "How about a yellow Pinto?" Like a trapper taking beaver pelts and buffalo skins from the wilds of the young country and delivering them to the sophisticated east, Shuler skinned two Pintos and hauled the pelts to Chicago and Connecticut.

DUSTIN SHULER
Car Pelt on Hamden Plaza sign

DUSTIN SHULER
Pinto Pelt

"Rain or shine—especially shine—the shimmering sparkle of Clyde Lynds' conversion of decorative and ordinary elements into an aesthetic object—a thing of beauty—cannot fail to dazzle your eyes. Behold—Pure Beauty!"
—DWB

Above:
CLYDE LYNDS
Sun Dog
1988

Right:
JAMES SEAWRIGHT
Magic Mirror
1984

"One last thing needs to be said. Your energetic and total commitment to us and our work, David, has not only renewed our commitment to it, but given us hope that it will be seen in our lifetimes as work that is some of the most important being done today. Your efforts must seem thankless at times, as ours do to us, but I have no doubt that the future will redeem it all."

—Letter from Clyde to DWB, October 1981

FREEDOM OF SPEECH *DOES* INCLUDE ART!

. . . even though government officials try to restrict that freedom by resorting to their zoning and permit regulations, sign ordinances, and other bureaucratic means.

Ad or Art? A Connecticut Court Must Say If Statute Covers Statue

By RICHARD L. MADDEN

Special to The New York Times

BRIDGEPORT, Conn., April 13 — For an hour today, Connecticut's highest court listened to arguments on whether a 32-foot-tall sculpture was a work of art, or merely a sign.

A sign, said a lawyer for the Town of Hamden, which has twice rejected applications by a shopping center, Hamden Plaza, to put the sculpture at an entrance along a busy stretch of Dixwell Avenue that is locally known as the "Magic Mile."

Art, said lawyers for the plaza's owners, who contend that the sculpture is protected by the First Amendment guarantee of free speech and cannot be barred from private property by a town ordinance that regulates the size of signs.

Copyright © 1988 by The New York Times Company. Reprinted by permission

The kinetic sculpture as pictured to the right by Harold Lehr was on display on the lawn of Wadsworth Atheneum for nearly a year. The Town refused to recognize its artistic value or the owners right to display it. It "became a sign" when placed in front of the shopping center, an attempt to use sign regulations to censor the choice of art to be displayed.

At considerable expense, the owners turned to the courts to protect their constitutional right to display art works of their choosing on their private property.

Seven years later, five judges in the Connecticut Supreme Court, the state's highest tribunal, unanimously agreed with the owner's position.

"Isn't it a terrible waste of money?"
"Good art is never a waste of money"
—DWB,
"A Guide to Puzzled Customers"

"Nobody wanted Ghost Parking Lot around. Everybody thought it was just terrible. Not David. The tenants didn't like it. The Village of Hamden didn't like it. It stayed right there, and he loved it. He thought it was just great."

—Bob Bermant (DWB's brother)

GHOST PARKING LOT

Memo from DWB to Hamden Plaza Tenants

I am aware that many of you are unable to explain to your customers what in the world I am doing with those junk cars along Dixwell Avenue. I suppose you might just say that I prefer them to the untidy debris and black emptiness I usually see there, but I guess I can do better. It's a lot of dough to spend just to "tidy up" an area. So, I have prepared a series of questions and answers that may be helpful to you.

Incidentally, inasmuch as this is still (thank God) a democracy, I can't and don't expect all of you to love what I am doing or agree with its concept or even welcome its presence. But I would hope that you will at least present my viewpoint to your customers—and yourselves.

"The true masterpiece at Hamden Plaza is SITE's 'Ghost Parking Lot', a huge sculptural installation built for and in the parking lot. The work integrates the aesthetic and sociological setting perfectly. It functions on many levels and informs the site. However, more than the formal integration of line, texture, materials, 'Ghost Parking Lot' addresses the actual social use of the site."

—Tom Finkelpearl

"The art critic (John Russell quoting John Cage) says, 'The function of art is to awaken us to the very life we live.' "

—DWB, "A Guide to Puzzled Customers"

LONG RIDGE MALL

WHY ART IN A SHOPPING CENTER?

By David Bermant, February 1970

Contemporary art (or more simply, the art being done today) has many facets and trends, most of them bewildering. Pop Art, Op Art, Minimal Art, Abstract Expressionism, Anti-Art, Earth Art—you name it and someone's doing it. It would be impossible even to list all these directions in the space allotted for this commentary. For Long Ridge Mall, I have selected the trend that interests me most, which might be called "Technological Art."

To put it as simply as possible, Technological Art is the application of today's scientific discoveries—be they materials, relationships, or principles—to produce objects of art. For example, the television screen of Nam June Paik is used as a canvas was by earlier artists; instead of paints, palette knife or brush, Paik uses colors and forms produced electronically on a television screen. As in much of this art, however, the end result is influenced by the actions of the viewer—in Paik's case by sounds—projected by the viewer into microphones attached to the set.

Many technological artists are engineers, scientists, or professors of art versed in electronic mechanics or skilled craftsmen with various aptitudes, but all share one goal: the production of a thing of beauty. Although the materials—plexiglass, strobe lights, aluminum, polarized glass, polyethylene, electronic sounds and devices, light images, etc.—may differ, and the scientific principles—optics, relativity, kinetics, cybernetics, etc.—may vary, the objective remains the same. Beauty, it has been said, is in the eye of the beholder. You may well differ with me as to the end result, but the means and the effort should nevertheless be of interest to you.

I believe that the workday human environment can stand some beautification. Why should the beauty of art be limited to special trips to a museum or art gallery, or to the fortunate few who can afford private collections in their homes? The primary function of Long Ridge Mall is of course to serve your shopping needs, but the presence of contemporary artworks of high quality cannot fail to enhance your daily life.

There may be no great works of art in this collection—no El Grecos, Rembrandts, or Picassos to move your spirit or religious sense. Yet there should be some that will bring a smile to your lips, a "wow" to your throat, or simply a feeling of pleasure at an idea well realized. The test of an artwork, for me, is simply that it makes me feel good. If you respond to any of these in the same way, that is sufficient.

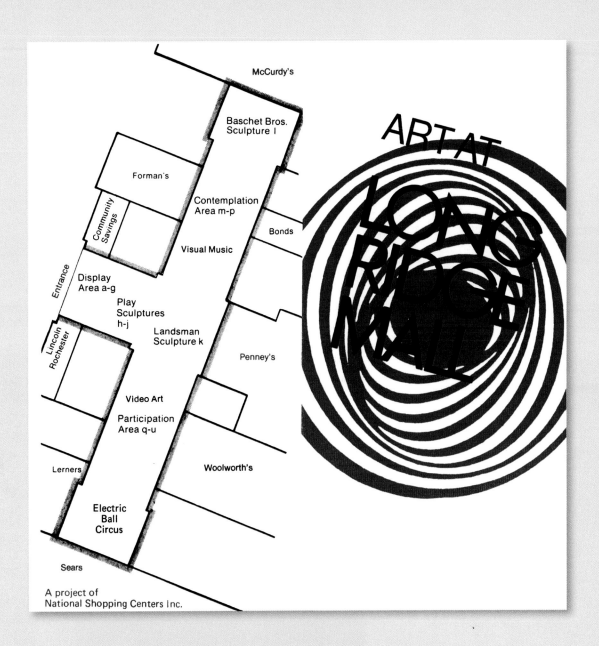

McCurdy's

Baschet Bros.
Sculpture l

Forman's

Community
Savings

Contemplation
Area m-p

Bonds

Visual Music

Entrance

Display
Area a-g

Play
Sculptures
h-j

Landsman
Sculpture k

Penney's

Lincoln
Rochester

Video Art

Participation
Area q-u

Lerners

Woolworth's

Electric
Ball
Circus

Sears

A project of
National Shopping Centers Inc.

ART AT
LONG
RIDGE
MALL

"Lighthouse is a wind sculpture, greeting shoppers at Long Ridge Mall with color and movement. At night an orbiting beacon of light is projected which is powered by the wind. A solar electrical system rotates the beacon if there is no wind."
—DWB

HAROLD LEHR
Lighthouse
1979

ELECTRIC BALL CIRCUS

A smile is the most prevalent facial expression among viewers of George Rhoads' sculptures. "Electric Ball Circus" is just that—a CIRCUS of sights and sounds, of colors and movements, of actions and reactions—the most colossal, exciting, funny art sculpture in the whole wide world!!! And you can participate . . . Ring a bell . . . Blow a whistle . . . Sound the thunder gong!

A painter and sculptor, George Rhoads started at a tender age being a clock-parts freak, and just went on from there—entranced with timing mechanisms that activated motor elements, making things make noise, and bending gravity to his sense of humor. Perhaps the comic drawings of Rube Goldberg form some of the inspiration of Rhoads' audio-kinetic inventions, and the interaction of machine and visitor is one of his primary goals. "People generally have a cheerful response," he says, "and children stand for hours looking at the sculptures."

George Rhoads' love of machines is very apparent in his sculptures. He feels machines have been mistreated by society, which may be part of the reason he pays them homage in his works. "Electric Ball Circus" took Rhoads nine months to construct, and he was assisted by Jerry Wolff of Slaterville Springs, New York.

"My sculpture at Long Ridge Mall was not popular with some people. When I was there installing it I encountered this kind of thing. People were shocked. I think it was simply the concept, the newness of it. I think most of the people who came to the mall hadn't even encountered modern art."

—George Rhoads

PAINTING OF LONG RIDGE MALL

H.N. Han

Long Ridge Mall in Greece, New York, was the only indoor shopping mall that David Bermant developed, and it housed the most extensive collection of the technological art he so loved.

H.N. HAN
Long Ridge painting detail
1976

"Is the purpose of public art to benefit the artist or the community? Obviously there is an ingredient that must be considered in the placing of public art that I believe has been ignored until now: the public! After all, public space is owned by the public, the art that's there has been paid for by the public, and most important, that very space is occupied by the public. Consequently, the emphasis upon 'site specific' should be shifted to another kind of specific: PEOPLE SPECIFIC."

DWB

JOHN HARRIS
Skywriting Tic Tac Toe
1971

Upon observing the exuberance with which children attack "Play Loaves," one knows that the artist is still a child at heart. It is a piece that feeds and interacts with children's rich imaginations most successfully.

JOHN HARRIS
Play Loaves
1972

BASCHET BROTHERS
Art at Long Ridge Mall Brochure

Francois and Bernard Baschet were born in Paris, in 1920 and 1917 respectively. The brothers have exhibited their acoustic artwork in numerous exhibitions around the world.

Francois Baschet has written: "My brother Bernard and I want to make a synthesis of these elements:

"Shapes – Acoustical laws are precise, some families of shapes are good, some are bad. Our metal surfaces can be compared to sails, but with a satisfactory acoustical ratio. We try to combine the aesthetic with the functional.

"Sounds – Possibilities in relating sound to form are immense. The chords have to be carefully programmed so that the sounds are not offensive.

"Public Participation – We feel that in our present-day computer card civilization the public must find new ways of expression. Whenever possible we invite the public to play. Reactions are very diverse. I encountered about ten tall, handsome, serious Swedes in a Scandinavian museum in a room full of people and our sculptures. They were motionless as they watched the crowd. 'Are you looking at the structures?' I asked. 'No,' they said. 'We are watching the public. We have never seen so many Swedes so happy without being drunk.' "

BASCHET BROTHERS
Musical Fountain
1974
58"H x 38"W

EXCERPT FROM *SOUND SCULPTURES* BY FRANCOIS & BERNARD BASCHET
By Francois Baschet, 1999
(Translated from French)

We constructed, with Terese Braunstein-Baudin, a monumental assembly of conical reservoirs emptied by siphons. The water, flowing in haphazard, unpredictable current, turned propellers, which in turn, made bells ring. David loved the fountain. He liked me as well and the feeling was mutual. He asked me to become his partner in a company specializing in the construction of sound fountains in the U.S., and perhaps the entire world. According to David, we would make a lot of money.

Once again, I found myself in one of those moments when one is a master of one's fate at a crossroads in life where everything is at stake. Instinct, not reason, made me refuse. But why?

Was it having read the book *The Protestant Ethic Spirit* written in 1895 by Max Weber? For the Protestants, as Franklin said, "Time is money." One praises the Lord by working as hard as he can. Stress is the road to heaven. To work, to earn money is to pray. As far as the glorification of the soul goes, a good nap that allows one to meditate on the uselessness of money, is worth eight hours of sweating in a factory. Thus, through laziness, I passed up American fame and fortune, preferring the sunsets over the Seine that turn Notre Dame from grey to gold. Amen.

SUCCESSFUL PUBLIC ART: IS IT POSSIBLE?

By David W. Bermant

1987

I have extensive experience with every aspect of placing art in public places. Here I present a sampling in words and pictures of the more than one hundred "objects" I am responsible for in certain public areas of our country.

Many of them either move or have movement as their subject matter. Therefore, be aware that a photograph of a moving object rarely does justice to that object, and aesthetic objects especially suffer grievously—sometimes fatally—by being frozen by a camera.

At the Port Authority Bus Terminal, 42nd Street and 8th Avenue in New York City, artist George Rhoads has located his "42nd Street Ballroom." His works are easily the most popular artwork in each public area, whether shopping center, airport, or bus terminal. Since they are accessible (an art term meaning "easily understood") to anyone of any age, group, race, or economic class, they are the first art objects I introduce into my shopping centers. They bring smiles to anyone capable of smiling. Is bringing a smile to one's face in this complicated and anxiety–ridden world an unworthy objective of a fine art piece?

At Logan Airport, Boston, Massachusetts, James Seawright has installed a much expanded version of his "Mirror I." This is an array of 121 mirror-faced blocks six feet by six feet. The faces of the blocks are inclined at the precise angles necessary to direct all the mirror faces to a focal point eight feet in front of the center of the array.

Also at Logan are two new pieces by George Rhoads similar to, but different from, the Bus Terminal piece in New York City. I believe Rhoads is possibly the most underrated (in the art establishment) artist-genius in the United States today.

The hostility of the American public to the usual art forms foisted upon it in its public spaces is well documented, highlighted by the confrontation over Richard Serra's "Tilted Arc" sculpture at the Federal Building in New York City. That this controversy will go on seems likely.

Recent articles appearing in *Stroll* magazine (a publication of Creative Time, a public art organization) indicated that the experts remain confused as to the why's of this hostility, but even more mystified by its rectification.

The entire problem can be summed up by Alvin S. Lane's question during the Serra controversy: "Is the purpose of public art to benefit the artist or the community?" Obviously there is an ingredient that must be considered in the placing of public art that I believe has been ignored until now: the public! After all, the public space is owned by the public, the art that's there has been paid for by the public and, most important, that very space is occupied by the public. Consequently, the emphasis on "site specific" should be shifted to another kind of specific: PEOPLE SPECIFIC.

Continued disregard for the public's opinion can result in the partial or entire dismantling of the hard-earned "one percent for art" programs. The author of the *Stroll* magazine article spotlighted the recent elimination of the Tacoma, Washington, public art program by public referendum because of the outrage created by Stephen Antanakos' $272,000 neon artwork for Tacoma's Dome.

That artists are beginning to recognize that consideration of the audience is the one ingredient essential for successful public art is typified by remarks reproduced in the *Stroll* article: well-known public artist Siah Armajani states, " . . . if public art is beyond comprehension, then it's not part of life." Sculptor Scott Burton points out, "The important thing is to make art that is intelligible to a non-art audience." And Seattle artist Richard Posner states, "Art in public places needs to speak with (rather than at) the people who live and work there."

This, then, is the challenge. The solution? One can be found in the use of materials by artists that are easily recognizable by a non-art audience, materials that are transformed into aesthetic objects—from the ordinary to the extraordinary. A material quite familiar to the non-art audience happens to be the product of the one feature unique to our society, distinguishing it from any previous society: technology.

Today's technological artist uses the technology of our day to create his or her aesthetic effect. The resulting art form uses, besides technology's materials, its theories and byproducts; it celebrates, criticizes and even pokes fun at it. The nontraditional materials it uses widen the scope of the subject matter of the visual arts, incorporating the very stuff of everyday living. How appropriate that it should be placed in everyday places!

(continued on page 124)

PUBLIC ART

GOLETA BEACH

GEORGE RHOADS
Windamajig
1991
180"H x 76" diameter
Goleta, California

"George Rhoads is the most appropriate work for public spaces . . . it makes a better day for people no matter who they are—rich or poor, educated or not. They get enjoyment out of it, talk about it, and then others come out to see it too."
—DWB

(continued)

However, describing this art form as technological is taboo when it is included in publicly owned places, as the museum world (whose approval is needed before panel participants choose art in public competitions) recalls the technological and kinetic art movements of the past as failed. Therefore, a new label has been suggested by Tom Finkelpearl: P.U.L.S.E. (People Using Light, Sound, Energy). The art world seems to require short labels to designate the art movement of the moment. It provides the curator, the art writer, and the art historian with a simplified code—to this writer a form of intellectual laziness, if not arrogance. Hence, the new name which I shall define as the use by artists of those forms, objects, materials, theories, etc. that come out of the technology and science of our day and are transformed by them into aesthetic expression.

The fact that such scientific origins produce movement in most cases—not all—is most felicitous for publicly placed art, since the viewer sees a different aspect of the art at each visit. Nam June Paik's television images are ever changing, and the colors and exact forms are never identical. This characteristic of P.U.L.S.E. keeps it fresh and new, eliminating the need to replace the art piece after it's been on display for a time. Go test it yourself. Go to the Bus Terminal in Manhattan at 42nd Street and 8th Avenue and walk until you see a crowd of people (all day long) gathered around a glass cube designed by George Rhoads, containing the traveling billiard balls producing sounds and movement. We all recognize billiard

(continued on page 126)

Letter From
Justin Ruhge

David Bermant

REC'D SB COUNTY PARK DEPT.
MAY -2 1991

P. O. Box 2216
Goleta, CA 93118
April 30, 1991

Mr. Mike Pahos, Director
Santa Barbara County Parks Department
610 Mission Canyon Road
Santa Barbara, CA 93105

Dear Mr. Pahos:

Please leave the art object at Goleta Beach. Where else is there such a thing? Besides it's interesting to watch and I believe it has aesthetic value.

In a world of nay-sayers, I am a yea-sayer.

Sincerely,

Justin Ruhge

Justin Ruhge
Goleta

cc: W. Wallace

PUBLIC ART

CIRCUIT

KENNY SCHNEIDER
Icarus Rides Again
1995
103"H x 90"W x 48"D
Ledbetter Beach
Santa Barbara, California

CIRCUIT

Circuit was a program created by DWB to promote public art. The David Bermant Foundation provided funds to museums and municipalities nationwide for the installation of a "bendable flagpole" which was used to display a series of wind pieces created by various artists. The wind pieces were lent by the Foundation and each piece stayed in place for six months before being replaced with a different piece for another six months.

(continued)

balls and most of us recognize the tongue-in-cheek comments on our machine age represented by the "happenings" produced by the action of the billiard balls. On the other hand, to view the usual public art form chosen by the cognoscenti, go to Lincoln Center in New York City and view the Henry Moore sculpture. See how many people sitting or walking around it actually look at it. They are people-watching or reading or drawing—anything but looking at the piece. Why? It's the same as it was before. And they don't truly understand what it is.

I don't recall ever seeing Henry Moore's name anywhere in the vicinity of his sculpture, never mind an explanation of what it's all about. Both are musts for public art. A non-art audience is entitled to know the identity of the artist and to receive an explanation of the work in terms that are understandable. In the art that I place in my shopping centers, I describe my understanding of what the art is about in such terms and include a short biography of the artist as well as a summary of art institutions in which the artist's work has been collected or exhibited. I have the artist check the copy before it's printed on a permanent sign placed near the artwork. This sign gives the general public some indication of what they're looking at and at the same time conveys an important message: "This is Art with a capital A. Please consider and respect it as such. Restrain yourself from vandalizing it and stop others from doing so." This works, most of the time.

*"My foundation is sponsoring what
I hope will be a landmark exhibition
of works focusing on the light and
movement aspects of this aesthetic
movement. It is scheduled to be held at
420 West Broadway in New York City,
opening on April 4, 1987. Its objective
is to inform the art world of the presence
of P.U.L.S.E., of its vitality and of its
superb aesthetic quality.*

*"I have been invited to curate an
exhibition at the MIT Museum in
Cambridge, Massachusetts, and I have
accepted subject to one condition: that
the works are located not only in the
museum but placed in the ordinary
everyday environment of the campus and
buildings of this technologically oriented
university. It is my hope that such an
exhibition will convince the art world
of the desirability of the use of this art
form in American public places."*

GEORGE RHOADS
Bee Tree (Circuit)
Wichita State University
1991

PUBLIC ART

UC SANTA BARBARA

"Please accept my heartfelt thanks for your allowing me and other UCSB faculty to have a glimpse of your very impressive collection of technological art.

"It also became very clear to me how fitting it is that this art should be 'art for public space.' It is indeed art that engages us all, helps summon our imaginations, and lets us view the world with new vision. I feel very fortunate to have had a glimpse into your world."

—*Evelyn Hu, Professor, Department of Electrical & Computer Engineering, UCSB, July 1997*

DWB with PETER LOGAN'S "Flying Pencils" at UCSB

UNIVERSITY OF CALIFORNIA, SANTA BARBARA

BERKELEY · DAVIS · IRVINE · LOS ANGELES · RIVERSIDE · SAN DIEGO · SAN FRANCISCO SANTA BARBARA · SANTA CRUZ

UNIVERSITY ART MUSEUM

SANTA BARBARA, CALIFORNIA 93106-7130
(805) 893-2951
FAX (805) 893-3013

December 16, 1996

Mr. David Bermant
1104 La Vista Road
Santa Barbara, CA 93110

Dear David:

I am writing to personally thank you for your recent gift of *Pencils* by Peter Logan, which was just installed on campus. The sculpture looks wonderful and is a perfect piece for a university setting with its combination of wit, good design, and intriguing motion. Everyone I have spoken with has commented on how appropriate it is and how fabulous it looks. People just love it! Moreover, given my expectations based on photographs, I also was struck by how much better it looks in person. The colors are more intense, the scale more impressive, and the kinetic action much more interesting.

Thanks again, David, for your generosity and for enlivening our campus in this way. You have done so much to enhance the quality of public art at UCSB.

With very best wishes for the holidays, I am

Sincerely yours,

Marla C. Berns
Director

PUBLIC ART

SANTA BARBARA AIRPORT

DUSTIN SHULER
Albatross V
1995
18"H x 156"W x 80"D (on 20' pole)

"And today before taking off from Santa Barbara Airport I visited an old friend—the sculpture in the patio garden—with new appreciation, for now I know it to be part of a much larger collection."

—*Visitor to private collection, 2008*

DUSTIN SHULER DESCRIBES "ALBATROSS"

"David said to me, 'Listen kid, I'm doing this thing where I've got this 20-foot tall pole and I want sculptures on top of it that move with the wind. What do you got?' So I proposed a couple things to him. The wonderful thing about David was if he didn't like it, if it didn't work for him, he'd say, 'No. What else you got?' That, 'What else you got' was the most important thing. But he loved the Albatross and I made seven of them. He bought five. They're very beautiful, and actually the wingspan equals the great wandering albatross of the South Seas. That's why I call them that."

GEORGE RHOADS

Good Time Clock IV

In 1984, George Rhoads designed and constructed "Good Time Clock IV," a delightful mixed media sculpture with more than twenty moving balls and an electric motor. It has been exhibited at the Aldrich Museum, the Santa Barbara Museum of Art, and UC Santa Barbara; loaned to LaGuardia airport; and displayed in a shopping center. It was loaned to the Santa Barbara Airport in 1990 by DWB and has been enjoyed by hundreds of thousands of passengers since then. In 2011, "Good Time Clock IV" was refurbished by Creative Machines and is now on permanent display at Santa Barbara's new airport terminal.

GEORGE RHOADS
Good Time Clock IV
1984
72"H x 72"W x 36"D

DAVID BERMANT FOUNDATION

MISSION STATEMENT OF THE DAVID BERMANT FOUNDATION

The David Bermant Foundation: Color, Light, Motion was established in 1986 to encourage and advocate experimental visual art which draws its form, content and working materials from late twentieth-century technology.

Founded by David W. Bermant, who in 1965 began to build a collection that has become the preeminent private assemblage of work from this genre, the Foundation is devoted to fostering the efforts of artists working with non-traditional materials. These materials include physical sources of energy, light and sound, which are used in works that question and extend the boundaries of the visual arts.

The Foundation seeks also to cultivate public awareness of and appreciation for the synthesis of fine art and technology by supporting artists and institutions involved in the presentation, study, commission, collection, or exhibition of such work.

Clockwise:

DWB with cigar box
....
Group shot of artists
....
DWB & Susan Hopmans
....
Artist party on patio of Rye house
....
Clyde Lynds & James Seawright

The inspiration to form the David Bermant Foundation arose out of David's love of the artists and his passion for the works they created.

DAVID BERMANT
FOUNDATION

FOUNDATION GRANTS

KRISTIN JONES

Luminessence
Rome, Italy

Upon graduating from Yale University School of Art in 1983, Kristin Jones won a Fullbright Fellowship to Rome, Italy, to explore the many ways that fountains animate and focus public space. She was struck by the potential and abandon of the Tiber River, and she imagined awakening it with evocative contemporary art that could manifest its fluid dynamic energy.

Years later, in 2001, Jones returned to Rome with a Senior Fullbright Fellowship and a vision for a flexible matrix of thousands of points of light, responsive to the Tiber's current. The organic, submerged waveform would mirror the sinuous path of the river as it meandered through the city, appearing to swim upstream like a school of fish or a serpentine constellation, evoking the Roman legend of Asclepius, the ancient Greek god of healing. The luminous structure, which Jones titled "Luminessence," would reveal the energy of the Tiber, illuminating and articulating its flow.

The David Bermant Foundation: Color, Light, Motion, long-time supporters of Jones' work, provided a three-year challenge grant to help the artist make her vision a reality. With the foundation's support, an initial theoretical and mathematical study conducted by the Courant Institute at New York University brought together a team of Roman colleagues from the Fluid Dynamics Department of the Engineering School of the University of Rome. In 2007 Jones collaborated with architect Daniel K. Brown to produce "Luminalia," a serpentine line of one thousand candles which illuminated a half-kilometer of the river basin. TEVERETERNO is an ongoing project working to develop a global competition for the responsible and dynamic renewal of the Tiber River, developing realizable landscape and infrastructure measures to facilitate public access and conservation of the urban waterfront.

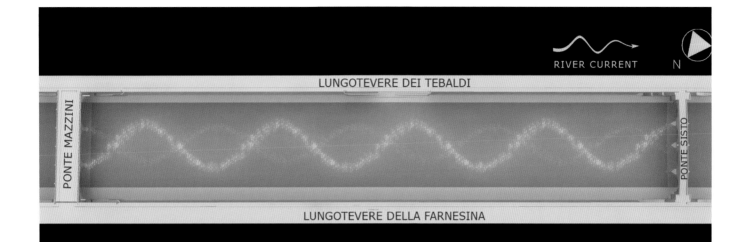

RIVER CURRENT   N

LUNGOTEVERE DEI TEBALDI

PONTE MAZZINI

PONTE SISTO

LUNGOTEVERE DELLA FARNESINA

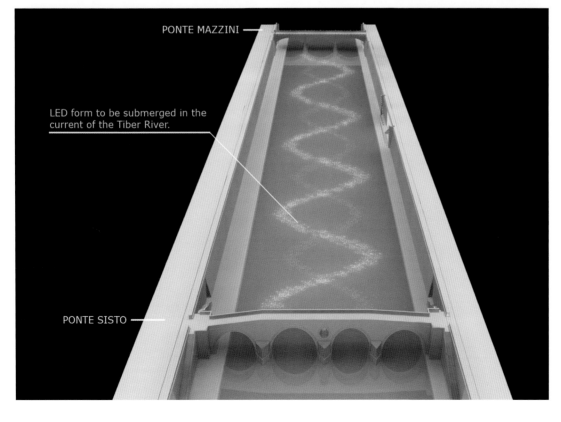

PONTE MAZZINI

LED form to be submerged in the current of the Tiber River.

PONTE SISTO

Employing the most current technology in LED lighting, "Luminessence" was conceived as a flexible model that could be adapted and transformed to multiple sites, drawing public attention to the plight and beauty of urban rivers internationally.

"David changed my life absolutely! His commitment to PUBLIC, to ART and to ARTISTS was so rigorous. David was a huge inspiration to me both by example and through our enormous differences. There was always a conquest, something new he was trying, or exploring: wine, art, even various diets and cures, bracelets, a new psychic . . . There was always a project in the air, a desire to be fulfilled to a greater and greater extent."

—*Kristin Jones*

DAVID BERMANT
FOUNDATION

FOUNDATION GRANTS

The Hudson River Museum
The Magic of Light
Yonkers, New York
2002

January 9, 2002

Ms. Sandra Powers
Secretary
The David Bermant Foundation: Color, Light, Motion
1104 La Vista Road
Santa Barbara, California 93110

Dear Ms. Powers:

On behalf of the Board of Trustees and staff of The Hudson River Museum, I am writing
to thank you for your generous grant of $5,000 in support of our upcoming exhibition *The
Magic of Light*. We are especially grateful for the extra effort you made to expedite the
funding process.

As you are aware, *The Magic of Light* will feature 18 works and site-specific installations
using artificial light. The show, which will open on February 1, is on schedule and
several of the site-specific pieces are already installed. We will send you installation
slides as soon as they are available, as well as a catalog.

Thank you again for your support. If anyone from the Foundation is planning on coming
to the New York area within the next couple of months, we would be more than happy to
welcome them to the Museum and take them on a tour. Please do not hesitate to contact
me at (914) 963-4550, extension 236, to arrange a visit.

Sincerely,

Michael Botwinick
Director

DAVID BERMANT
FOUNDATION

FOUNDATION GRANTS

LUKE SAVISKY
I of Texas
First Night Austin
Austin, Texas
2007

April 2, 2007

Ms. Sandy Hopmans
The David Bermant Foundation
1104 La Vista Rd.
Santa Barbara, CA 93110

Dear Sandy:

On behalf of First Night Austin, I would like to thank you for The David Bermant Foundation's donation in the amount of $10,000 to First Night Austin 2007. As you know, First Night Austin is a 501c3 organization that relies solely on the support and generosity of our sponsors.

The Luke Savisky projection project sponsored by the David Bermant Foundation was easily one of the top two most popular projects and was featured on the cover the Austin Chronicle. We are sending you a thank you package that includes an original copy of the coverage. I will also send you photos by email.

With your support, First Night Austin 2007 saw a continuation of the enormous success of its inaugural year in 2006, with a 30% increase in attendees, bringing the total count to well over 130,000 citizens. We expect an even larger audience for First Night Austin 2008 and look forward to the David Bermant Foundation's continued support as a project sponsor.

First Night gives Austin the opportunity to appreciate the visual and performing arts through a diverse and high-quality New Year's Eve program that provides a shared cultural experience that is accessible and free to all. First Night celebrates the artist in all of us and a community that values the drive to create.

Thanks to your generosity, First Night Austin will continue to grow as a family-friendly Austin tradition.

Sincerely,

Ginny Sanders
Executive Director
First Night Austin

DAVID BERMANT
FOUNDATION

FOUNDATION GRANTS

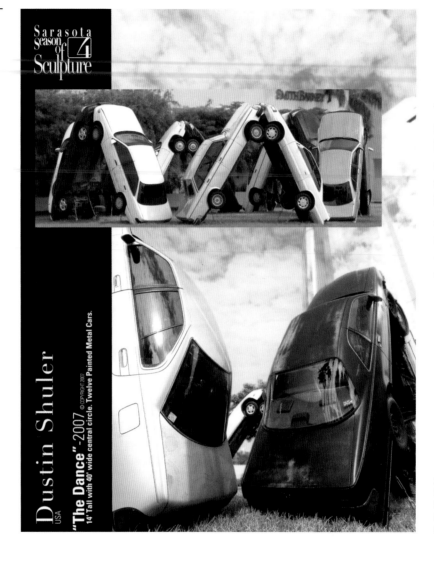

Sarasota
Season
of 4
Sculpture

Dustin Shuler USA
"The Dance" - 2007 © COPYRIGHT 2007
14' Tall with 40' wide central circle. Twelve Painted Metal Cars.

SMITH BARNEY

"The sculptures your grant sponsored have been such a hit, especially Dustin's piece which has generated a lot of dialogue."

—*Brenda Terris,
Executive Director,
Sarasota Season of
Sculpture*

*DUSTIN SHULER
The Dance
Sarasota Season of Sculpture
Sarasota, Florida
2007*

"The Dance"-2007 © COPYRIGHT 2007

14' Tall with 40' wide central circle. Twelve Painted Metal Cars.
"To me cars are an ancient dream come true; a magic carpet to take us wherever we wish to go. I know that cars could be and will be better and cleaner than they are now, but so far, this is the closest we have gotten to that magic carpet. Therefore I have created the magic "Dance" of the cars."

Selected Exhibitions:
2000
Patricia Correia Gallery
1998
"Vehicles Transcending the Millenium", Los Angeles, CA
1997-99
"Elusive Paradise", An installation designed and curated by John Otterbridge, The Geffen Contemporary at MOCA, Los Angeles, CA
1997
"Through the Looking Glass", Cypress College Fine arts Gallery, Cypress, CA
1996
"California Index 17", Merging One Gallery, Santa Monica, CA
1996
"Facing the Dragon", Artopia Gallery, Hollywood, CA
1992
"Hot August Nights", Nevada Museum of Art", Reno NV
1991
"Status of Sculpture", Lowen Palace, Berlin, Germany
1989
"The Road Show", John Michael Kohler Arts Center, Sheboygan, WI
1989
"The Traveling Show, Art Influenced by Transportation",
Muckenthaler Cultural Center, Fuller, CA
1985
"Cowboys, Cadillacs and Computers", Lawndale Annex,
University of Houston, TX
1983
"Irvine Collects", Irvine Cultural Center, Irvine, CA
1980
"Architectural Sculpture", Los Angeles Institute of Contemporary Art

Selected Commissions:
1998
"Batross VII", Collection of the Edwin A Ulrich Museum of Art, Wichita State University, Wichita, KS
1990
"The Sea Bee", Allendale Plaza, Coltsville, MA
1989
"Spindle", Cermak Plaza, Berwyn, IL
1988
"Yellow Pinto Pelt", Cermak Plaza, Berwyn, IL
1988
"Green Pinto Pelt", Hamden Plaza, Hamden, CT
1987
"Saab Pelt", University of Connecticut at Avery Point, Groton, CT
1987
"Triumph Pelt", San Jose Dept. of Motor Vehicles, San Jose, CA
1985
"Spider Pelt" San Francisco Arts Commission, San Francisco, CA
1982
"Pinned: Aircraft as Butterfly", American Hotel, Los Angeles, CA
1980
"Death of an Era", California State University, Dominguez Hills, CA

Selected Publications:
Sculpture Magazine
Harper's Magazine
Vanity Fair
The Wall Street Journal
People Magazine

Education:
1967-70
Carnegie Institute of Technology, Pittsburgh, PA

LEAD SPONSOR
Publix.

EXHIBITION SPONSOR
LEXUS
WILDE LEXUS OF SARASOTA

INFORMATION SPONSOR
ROBERTA LEVENTHAL SUDAKOFF *foundation*

Sarasota season of Sculpture

941.366.7767
www.seasonofsculpture.com

Photography by Gene Pollux, Pollux Photography / Graphic Design by Toby Thompson

FOUNDATION GRANTS

VICTORIA VESNA

Nanomandala

Nanomandala is an installation by media artist Victoria Vesna, in collaboration with nanoscience pioneer, James Gimzewski. On a bed of sand eight feet in diameter, a video of images is projected in evolving scale, from a microscopic view of the surface of a single grain of sand (achieved with a scanning electron microscope), to an image of the complete mandala. This coming together of art,

science, and technology is a modern interpretation of an ancient tradition that consecrates the planet and its inhabitants to bring about purification and healing. The sand mandala of Chakrasamvara represented in this installation was originally created by Tibetan Buddhist monks from the Gaden Lhopa Khangtsen Monastery in India, for the "Circle of Bliss" exhibition on Nepalese and Tibetan Buddhist Art at the Los Angeles County Museum of Art in 2003. This was the first time this particular sand mandala had been made in the United States.

ART | SCI

2009

"I can't thank you enough for allowing my drawing class the very special privilege of seeing the collection. We couldn't stop talking about it. Our instructor was so inspired that our next assignment is to draw a large mandala."

—Gallery visitor

DAVID BERMANT
FOUNDATION

FOUNDATION GRANTS

NAM JUNE PAIK
Ruin (2001)
Sensory Overload
Milwaukee Art Museum
2008–2009

MILWAUKEE ART MUSEUM

April 7, 2008

Sandra M. Hopmans
1104 La Vista Road
Santa Barbra, CA 93110

Dear Ms. Hopmans,

Thank you for your generous gift for the *Sensory Overload: Light, Motion, Sound, and
the Optical in Art Since 1945* held at the Milwaukee Art Museum January 24, 2008 –
October 1, 2009. As you might know, we restored and installed difficult materials for our
exhibition and we are grateful for your support.

My visit to see The David Bermant Collection at Susan's home was enjoyable and I was
pleased to see parallels with the Milwaukee Art Museum's collection. It was a treat to see
such outstanding examples in the collection such as Jam Jun Paik's *Virtually Wise* and
Otto Piene's *Light Ballet I.*

The *Sensory Overload* exhibition has proven to be a great success. It has attracted local
and national attention just as *Light/Motion/Space* did in 1967. We look forward to
working with the Foundation to determine how you will be credited on forthcoming
exhibition materials.

Sincerely,

Joseph D. Ketner II
Chief Curator

JK/dp

FOUNDATION GRANTS

UNIVERSITY OF CALIFORNIA, SANTA BARBARA

Kavli Institute for Theoretical Physics
Ulysses (1999–2009)

Jean-Pierre Hébert has created these acclaimed sand gardens blending modern technology and timeless spirituality. A quiet ball in slow, magical motion creates beautiful, ephemeral traces on the sand, as each drawing erases the previous one, echoing the Buddhist awareness of impermanence and the wheel of life.

"Picture a sand garden in the spirit of the Zen gardens of Japan. Only sand in a simple frame of beautiful wood. Hidden, a discreet digital system conducive to meditation, peace and serenity. Visible, the modest sand where beauty and nature stroll hand in hand through the rhythm of human existence . . . "

—Jean-Pierre Hébert

"It was a special privilege for me to be able to thank you in person during your recent visit, for the generous support of the David Bermant Foundation that has made it possible for so many to enjoy this remarkable piece in what feels like its natural home."

—David Gross to Susan Hopmans, July 6, 2009

KAVLI INSTITUTE FOR THEORETICAL PHYSICS

UNIVERSITY OF CALIFORNIA
SANTA BARBARA, CALIFORNIA 93106-4030
http://www.kitp.ucsb.edu

TELEPHONE: (805) 893-4111
TELEFAX: (805) 893-2431
gross@kitp.ucsb.edu

July 6, 2009

Susan Hopmans
The David Bermant Foundation
1104 La Vista Road
Santa Barbara, CA 93110

Dear Susan,

I write to thank you for your wonderful support of KITP Artist-in-Residence, Jean-Pierre Hebert. The David Bermant Foundation is a pioneer in fostering and featuring work that draws inspiration from both art and science, and I have always considered Jean-Pierre a visionary in this field as well. We have benefitted tremendously from his collaborations at the institute with many of its distinguished visitors and with other colleagues he has invited to campus.

As I said in my remarks during your recent visit, it was many years ago that I first saw Jean-Pierre's sculpture, now called *Ulysses,* and instinctively knew this piece would be an unusually perfect fit for the institute in its beautiful Michael Grave home. *Ulysses* fascinates scientists and other visitors alike as a result of its mathematical, artistic and almost Zen-like qualities. We host over a thousand visitors a year at the institute from around the world, some of the brightest minds in science, and each visitor inevitably pauses by *Ulysses.* Jean-Pierre's 'sand machine' by the institute's grand staircase simultaneously offers stimulation and moments for contemplation, all too rare in a fast-paced world.

It was a special privilege for me to be able to thank you in person during your recent visit, for the generous support of the David Bermant Foundation that has made it possible for so many to enjoy this remarkable piece in what feels like its natural home. Any time you wish to visit please let us know so we can facilitate things for you and your guests. Thank you for your invitation to visit the Collection this summer, and for your kind offer of dinner . I look forward to this visit, and to having you join us from time to time as our *Art, Image and Science Initiative* continues to foster valuable interactions between art and science.

Best wishes,

David Gross
Director
Frederick W. Gluck Professor of Theoretical Physics

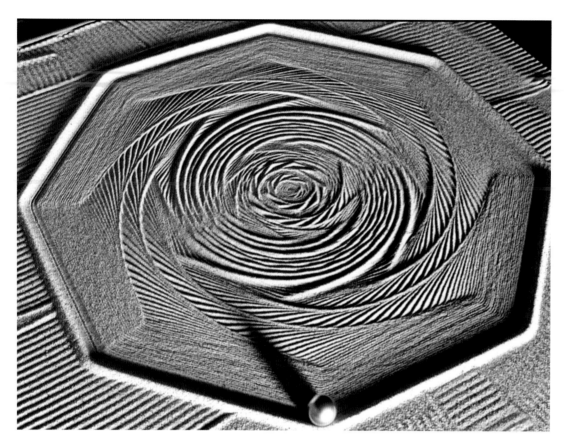

"The David Bermant Foundation is a pioneer in fostering and featuring work that draws inspiration from both art and science."

—David Gross
Director, KAVLI Institute

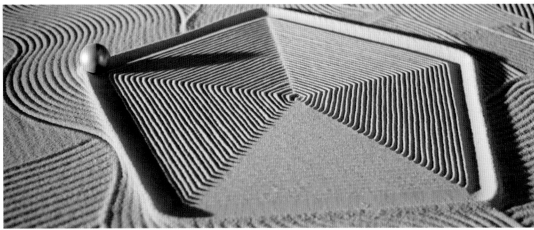

DAVID BERMANT
FOUNDATION

FOUNDATION GRANTS

BLUE MORPH

Spring Equinox:

March 20, 2010

Theater DoZ,Santa Ynez, CA

VICTORIA VESNA
JAMES GIMZEWSKI

BLUE MORPH

date: Spring Equinox: March 20, 2010
time: 6:30pm -- midnight
venue: Theater DoZ
3630-H Sagunto Street
Santa Ynez CA 93460
contact: 805-688-1372

Nanotechnology is changing our perception of life and this is symbolic in **the Blue Morpho butterfly** with the optics involved -- that beautiful blue color is not pigment at all but patterns and structure which is what nano-photonics is centered on studying. The optics are no doubt fascinating but the real surprise is in the discovery of the way cellular change takes place in a butterfly. Sounds of metamorphosis are not gradual or even that pleasant as we would imagine it. Rather the cellular transformation happens in sudden surges that are broken up with stillness and silence. The audience is invited to immerse themselves in the sounds of metamorphosis and be the performer in the piece.

ONGOING METAMORPHOSIS BY
MEDIA ARTIST VICTORIA VESNA
NANOSCIENTIST JAMES GIMZEWSKI

GUEST: LEAS MARIA
COLLABORATORS: MIU LING LAM, ROMIE LITRELL, BLANKA BUIC, PINAR YOLDAS

Special thanks to Susan Hopmans and the David Bermant Foundation for their continuous support.

http://artsci.ucla.edu/BlueMorph

 ART|SCI   C (N) S I

FOUNDATION GRANTS

AN OUTDOOR SCULPTURE EXHIBITION OF SOUND & MOTION

WIND *through the* TREES

"Three Moons Rising" by Jeff Kahn

October 2010 *through* June 2011

**65 sculptures featuring sound & movement
in a 15 acre botanical setting**

Don't miss this one-of-a-kind exhibition
at Jenkins Arboretum & Gardens!

Call **610.647.8870** *or visit*
www.jenkinsarboretum.org
for more information.

Jenkins Arboretum
& Gardens

*REIN TRIEFELDT
Flyer (2010)
Wind through the Trees
Jenkins Arboretum
Devon, Pennsylvania
2010–2011*

"We are delighted to have the David Bermant
Foundation among our supporters for 'Wind in the
Trees.' The exhibition has been completely installed
and includes 49 kinetic and auditory sculpture
installations involving 65 component works. We
think it is a very impressive body of work and
we've already received a great deal of publicity.
Thank you again for your generous grant."

*—Harold Sweetman
Executive Director, Jenkins Arboretum*

PROJECTS FOR A NEW MILLENIUM

Joy Wulke, Founder/Creative Director

"We greatly appreciate your contribution to support 'Terra Mirabila,' celebrating our 10th anniversary of phantasmagorical quarry projects. Our audiences are coming from New York, Massachusetts, Rhode Island, and Connecticut. We used our magic recipe of laser, theatrical light, water features, original score and poetry to illustrate our story. Your support has been critical and greatly appreciated during our eleven years of existence."

"Truly a triumph."

"Exciting and enchanting experience."

"The best yet, thank you for making it happen."

AFTERWORD

January 21, 1997

Memo To My Wife Susan Hopmans

Re: My desires as to funeral, services, etc. upon my death

Simply put, I would like to be cremated and my ashes placed in a urn (hopefully to be designed and constructed by Clyde Lynds) to be placed on or near his monolith at Santa Ynez, California entitled "ROSETTA SERIES, MOONSTONE I" 1982. If the artist fails to provide an urn, then a simple one of your choosing should be used and placed among the art collection, to remain with the collection in perpetuity.

I do not desire funeral services of a formal nature at the time of my death, but a simple gathering of my relatives and friends, and especially "my artists", approximately nine months following my death, I feel would be appropriate. At such a gathering stories concerning my relationships might be told. The service of some of my un-consumed wines should accompany the gathering. I wish to be remembered by the wonderful people who were part of my life.

David W. Bermant
David W. Bermant

Amelia M. Powers
Witness

Wendy K. Powers
Witness

✦ *This gathering will be held in Santa Barbara, September 16th 2000 ~ You are Cordially invited ~*

ART FOR PUBLIC SPACE
BERMANT ENTERPRISES, LTD.
NATIONAL SHOPPING CENTERS
DAVID BERMANT FOUNDATION: COLOR, LIGHT, MOTION

CLYDE LYNDS

20 Franklin Avenue
Wallington, New Jersey 07057
973 472-4653 Fax 973 472-0746

May 24, 2000

Dear Susan,

Enclosed you will find the drawings I've made for the urn. I apologize for the time it took, I had to have time to think clearly and too many emotions welled up earlier.

The Urn itself, of polished stainless steel, is made to resemble a shooting star in the form of an extruded Star of David. I felt the Star of David was particularly appropriate for several reasons. The first is his name, the second, his religion, and the other, equally important, is that he, like the biblical David, was never afraid to tackle the giant whether it was a person, project or cause. Nothing daunted him so the form made sense to me. Designing it like a shooting star, as if it were in movement also has obvious parallels to his life as you know.

He once told me, "Lynds, I'll tell you something about myself. If there were two pieces of art side by side and all things ere equal and one glittered and the other one didn't I'd pick the one that glittered." So would I.

The base is of polished black granite. The granite is a particular type that has small facets of quartz or mica imbedded in it. When it is polished it takes on a glitter in the sunlight, a kind of stardust effect, which I felt he would approve of.

I have sent a copy of the above description to Andy for his comments also. My time in designing and supervising production won't be charged for but I would ask that the estate pay for the fabrication and shipping. Let me know how you want me to proceed.

I hope you are well and that everything and every one around you is too.

My best,

Dear Susan:

It is with my deepest regrets that I apologize for not being with you on this special day. Family responsibilities prevented me from being able to travel to California to share my thoughts with you, but I feel a need to say the following about David.

David celebrated life and brought other along for the ride. His motivation to collect art was based solely upon his desire to share beauty with others. It was not about ego. It was not about elitism, rather, he drew inspiration from a genuine affection for his fellow man and from his desire to share the wonders of art and his passion for its uniqueness with others. Art truly did impact significantly the quality of his life and he genuinely wanted to share that discovery.

His unbridled passion for new media was seen by most of us as courageous. And it was. But to David, art based on technology was clearly no different than the art of the Renaissance. Great art is great art--no matter the path to its completion. In technologically inspired art, David realized what the art world is just beginning to discover--that art truly must reflect its time and environment. It has taken museums decades to finally acknowledge the achievement of the artists whom David collected and encouraged many, many years ago.

David Bermant was a visionary. With the curiosity of a child, coupled with the entrepreneurial brilliance that distinguished him in the world of business, he would create the first serious collection of the new art. And with evangelical zeal he went about the Herculean task of educating Americans that art can be built with electronic components--not just canvas and paint.

I believe with all my heart that when the final chapter is written on the art of our time, that David Bermant will be seen as a modern day Medici. We truly have lost a great man, but those of us who knew and admired him will forever be touched and enlivened by his spirit.

Lou

Lou Zona

Susan — I was recently going through a drawer of 'saved letters' and found a great note from David (Feb 1998). What a treasure it is.

I think of him often for it was David who introduced technological art to me. We have since the first showing of your beautiful collection — been very dedicated to technically oriented art. We even call one of our galleries — the David Bermant Gallery. Please come to visit.

We will be opening a show of Alejandro + Moira Sina in early December. It would be great to see you — with your blessing we will dedicate the show to David's memory. It promises to be a wonderful show.

All the best

THE BUTLER INSTITUTE OF AMERICAN ART · 524 WICK AVENUE · YOUNGSTOWN, OHIO 44502

Lou Zona

Who was that man with the magic cane and sparkling shirts? Urban myth or merry prankster? Did David Bermant exist or was he an illusion, a hologram, a light dancing through the shadows? Was he the developer, collector, promoter, philanthropist who some knew . . . or was he the fantasy, the illusion, the kinetic creation of some far out, laughing, jokester artist? At some level he will always bring joy to those of us lucky enough to live in Santa Barbara. We see his art at our libraries, universities, airport and beaches. His children and wife carry on his legacy of philanthropy and support for the arts. His thoughtful art collection is preserved and shown throughout the world. The man may be gone, the image may have disappeared, but the fun will continue forever.

"Pull this lever," he said, his eyes twinkling in expectation. "Pull this lever, you'll be amazed at the effect the artist has created." As I pulled up hard on the stainless steel lever a powerful stream of water shot from the sculpture, soaking my slacks. Laughing, David continued with the tour of his art collection. I still picture him as this Zen-like Yoda gazing out to sea from his hilltop sculpture garden. If you can imagine the whirling clocks, floating rocks and fiber optic illusions of this 20th century mind, you would be amazed to know he was also an army major, mall magnate and Yale cum laude. We were fortunate to have him in Santa Barbara. "The end of fine art is to produce a favorable impression upon the mind of the viewer." That was David's aesthetic . . . a mist retreating from the morning sun.

Steve Cushman
President, Santa Barbara Chamber of Commerce
Contemporary Arts Forum Board Member

"I do hope you have a curator or a guide taking you along on these art walks or you're gonna to be spending most of your time trying to find out how these damn things work. I hope my foundation left enough money so that we could employ people to assist those of you interested enough to come here to look at this art, assist you in seeing it. I'll never know. Fancy that."

DWB